MW00848496

I Am *Not* Defeated

10 Ways to Demolish Mental Demons

Doug Robins

Copyright © 2021 by **Doug Robins**

All rights reserved. No part of this publication may be reproduced, distributed, or transmitted in any form or by any means, without prior written permission.

Scripture quotations marked (ESV) are taken from The ESV® Bible (The Holy Bible, English Standard Version®) copyright © 2001 by Crossway, a publishing ministry of Good News Publishers. ESV® Text Edition: 2011. The ESV® text has been reproduced in cooperation with and by permission of Good News Publishers. Unauthorized reproduction of this publication is prohibited. Used by permission. All rights reserved.

Scripture quotations marked (NIV) are taken from the Holy Bible, New International Version. Copyright © 1973, 1978, 1984, 2011 by Biblica, Inc.® Used by permission. All rights reserved worldwide.

Scripture quotations marked (NLT) are taken from the Holy Bible, New Living Translation, copyright © 1996, 2004, 2015 by Tyndale House Foundation. Used by permission of Tyndale House Publishers, Inc., Carol Stream, Illinois 60188. All rights reserved.

Renown Publishing
www.renownpublishing.com

I Am Not Defeated / Doug Robins
ISBN-13: 978-1-952602-29-0

In dedication to my wife Jeannie Robins, Miriam Callahan, and Lorenzo Gomez. My beloved Jeannie works tirelessly to help people come to emotional and spiritual health. Miriam is a counselor and mentor who helped heal my marriage, and her fingerprints are throughout this book. Without Lorenzo's encouragement and inspiration, I might never have written these pages.

CONTENTS

Embrace the Perspective of a Cracked Pot

A water carrier in India would dip his clay pots into the stream for water, then carry those pots up to his house. He had two different clay pots. One pot was perfect, and this perfect pot never spilled a drop. The other pot had a crack, and it was never able to carry all the water that was put in it. The water would leak out onto the ground.

The perfect pot felt proud of its accomplishment: "I carried all the water up to the house!" The broken pot, the one with the crack in it, felt down about its contribution. "I only filled half my potential because of my brokenness."[1]

Do you ever feel like the broken pot? Do your problems or your depression or anxiety cause you to feel as if you aren't good enough, doing enough, offering enough? We can go down a long list of celebrities and artists that we lost in recent years to mental illness or brokenness. Robin Williams, a prolific actor; Anthony Bourdain, a renowned chef; Chris Cornell, the lead singer from Soundgarden; and Chester Bennington, the lead singer of Linkin Park—all took their own lives.

Our feelings of "not good enough" can lead us down very dark paths. I love the declaration that was made by the grieving son of Chester Bennington. After Bennington took his own life, his son Draven Bennington said, "I want to make a commitment that I will talk to someone before I hurt myself when I'm feeling depressed, sad, or going through a hard week, month, or year."[2] That is a great and powerful declaration. Seeking help before you choose to do something to hurt yourself is a brave and important way through the darkness.

We all want to deal with how we feel in an appropriate and healthy way, and talking to someone, seeking help, choosing to reach out is part of that solution. In doing this, we take control. We refuse to let the darkness win. We make a way toward healing.

Apostle Paul and Mental Health

The apostle Paul was a guy who had a fair amount of strong feelings. In 2 Corinthians 4:7–9, Paul said, "But we have this treasure in jars of clay to show that this all-surpassing power is from God and not from us. We are hard pressed on every side, but not crushed; perplexed, but not in despair; persecuted but not abandoned; struck down, but not destroyed" (NIV).

This is how Paul felt on the inside. He was a guy who saw all kinds of miraculous stuff happen in his life. God performed countless miracles in and through him. But Paul still struggled. He prayed specifically about a thorn in his flesh (2 Corinthians 12:7–8). It was a problem area, a "crack" in his pot. He longed to be free of this burden, and in 2 Corinthians 12:9, he received his answer. God said, "'My grace is sufficient for you, for my power is made perfect in weakness.' Therefore I will boast all the more gladly about my weaknesses, so that Christ's power may rest on me" (NIV).

Being Christian doesn't mean that we don't get cracks. It doesn't mean that we don't get depressed, anxious, or immersed in dark thoughts. But it *does* mean that we can allow those cracks in our lives to unleash the power of God in a greater, more miraculous way.

Spiritual Tune-Up

My first vehicle was a pickup truck. I was young and inexperienced at having a car, so I just liked to drive. I didn't worry about maintenance. I didn't worry about tune-ups. I didn't worry about oil changes. Everybody who has a car knows this story never ends well. I ended up on the side of the road, smoke pouring out of the hood of my pickup truck. I learned a very expensive lesson, at a time in my life when I didn't have the money to have an expensive lesson. I learned the importance of tune-ups.

This book is your next tune-up. It just might prevent you from ending up on the emotional and spiritual side of the road with smoke pouring out of your soul.

It just might be the one thing that helps you through whatever it is you're going through, because this book is going to offer a lot of encouragement.

That's what I want for you.

I want you to be encouraged so that you can identify that crack, that thorn. At the end of each chapter, workbook sections will give you guided questions and applications to help you take it to God and work through it, believing that His grace is sufficient. I want you to get your tune-up so that you can hit the road and continue to see how God works.

The Cracked Pot

Earlier, I told you about the water carrier and the cracked pot. Well, here's the rest of the story:

One day, the cracked pot spoke to his owner and said, "I am ashamed of myself, and I want to apologize that I have only been able to deliver half my water to your house. Because of my flaws, you don't get full value from your efforts." Then the water carrier replied: "As we return to the house, I want you to notice the beautiful flowers along the path."[3] On that trip from the stream, the cracked pot looked around. The water carrier said:

> "Did you notice there are flowers only on your side of the path, but not on the other pot's side? That's because I have always known about your flaw, and I took

advantage of it. I planted flower seeds on your side of the path, and every day while we walk back from the stream, you've watered them."[4]

For years, the water carrier had been able to pick those flowers to decorated his table—because of the cracks in the pot. Cracked pots have purpose, and that purpose has nothing to do with finding perfect healing or delivery or repair. There is purpose even in your hardest moments.

CHAPTER ONE

Embrace the Tools of Emotional Health

Most of us walk around with cracks in our pots, and this causes us to feel shame, anger, resentment, fear, and worse. These feelings can build up and affect how we live and treat those around us. They can affect our relationship with God too.

If we're ever going to learn how to live abundantly *in spite of* our cracks, then we first need to learn how to deal with the emotions that being a broken, imperfect human can bring. I have seven tools to help you do this.

Tool 1: Community and Connection

According to the book *Connecting* by Larry Crabb, this world-renowned Christian psychologist has made a radical shift regarding therapy. Rather than just doing psychological surgery through therapy, he has a vision to see psychological nutrition through *community* and *people connecting*. This does not mean he thinks therapy is something that is not needed—therapy will always be needed. But in his book, he says, "I am now working toward the day when communities of God's people, ordinary Christians whose lives regularly intersect, will accomplish most of the good we now depend on mental health professionals to provide. They will do it by connecting with each other in ways that only the gospel makes possible."[5]

He believes it's through community that we get the best emotional nutrition, and that a strong community can lessen the need for intensive therapy. He goes on to say, "The greatest need in modern civilization is the development of communities—true communities where the heart of God is home, where the humble and wise learn to shepherd those on the path behind them, where trusting strugglers lock arms with others as together they journey on."[6]

What if we became a community where other strugglers can come alongside, lock arms together, and give each other the emotional nutrition we need to work through our feelings and struggles? It's a powerful thought.

What if you were to reach out to your Christian

community the next time you find yourself drowning in feelings of anger, hurt, resentment, shame, or whatever you're dealing with? I am convinced that if we were all to come together with the purpose of helping one another emotionally and mentally, we would find the firm foundation that we so often seek through therapy, medication, and other avenues.

Tool 2: Conflict

The second way to deal with your feelings involves conflict. We all have that person in life who frustrates us. They may even traumatize us or control us. We know that this relationship is not helping us move forward, and yet it's so hard to move to action.

Consider this your green light.

If you are in a situation right now where someone is abusing or hurting you, get out.

If a relationship is causing stress or frustrations, talk to them.

Begin to take control of the relationships you're in, and you will find that you are then in more control of your feelings. By creating boundaries or even completely cutting off a relationship, you are preparing yourself for a healthier mental future.

Then, forgive. I'm not talking about forgiving and forgetting, welcoming the person back into your life—there are some people who should be permanently banned from your life. I'm talking about releasing the emotional baggage that you will undoubtedly carry after setting new boundaries, experiencing some freedom, and realizing exactly how bad the relationship was for a long time. While there are times we have to create boundaries that completely cut someone out of our lives, at other times, God does a miraculous work of relational healing, in which we're able to invite the forgiven person back into our lives to have a deep friendship.

One time when I was in California, a guy came up to me with a prophetic word. He explained to me how I'd been hurt by a leader under whom I had served a while back. He said, in a very encouraging way, that I was going to receive a spiritual promotion when I released the feelings I was holding against this person and forgave him.

I was deeply impacted by this, because he was right. I was allowing past hurts to impact my heart and ministry. Immediately, I sent that old ministry leader who had hurt me a text message, telling him I had forgiven him and that I still loved him. As soon as I did that, I felt an emotional release, and ever since that day, I haven't felt any resentment or baggage from that relationship. I'm free.

If you find yourself with an incessant need to vent to others, it is often a sign of unforgiveness. Do not ignore this warning sign. It's time to forgive! It's time to move on from the past and embrace the future. Yes, there are people you may need to cut out of your life permanently, but that doesn't mean you can't forgive them for the horrible things they did. Do so, and you will begin to regain control of your feelings.

Tool 3: Consciousness

The third way to deal with the way you feel involves your consciousness. This includes the thoughts and ideas that you allow to take root within your mind.

Dr. Daniel Amen's organization has examined over 83,000 brain scans. They have looked at the brain scans of NFL players who have been injured with concussions, as well as the brain scans of criminals in prison systems. In these studies, they have made a direct correlation between brain injuries, mental disorders (ADD, anxiety, depression, etc.), and criminal behaviors.[7]

Our brain is extremely sensitive! Just as a high-impact collision can affect our thoughts and therefore our actions, so can negative thoughts and attitudes. The things we think about matter.

The good news is that the brain can heal and become restored. When we guard our minds from negative self-talk and what I consider to be unconstructive self-criticism, then we soon find that our feelings improve.

The Bible knows this: "Finally, brothers and sisters, whatever is true, whatever is noble, whatever is right, whatever is pure, whatever is lovely, whatever is admirable—if anything is excellent or praiseworthy—think about such things" (Philippians 4:8 NIV).

And Romans 12:2 reads, "Do not conform to the pattern of this world, but be transformed by the renewing of your mind" (NIV).

To gain control of your feelings, you must first gain control of your consciousness. Renew your mind! Think upon good, pure things! And watch as you begin to experience healing.

Tool 4: Culture

The fourth tool to deal and work through your feelings involves your culture. Every place you go has a culture. Every school you've attended, every company you've worked for, every neighborhood you're in, every church you've called home. These unique environments create pockets of culture that shape you.

The question is: what messages are these pockets of culture telling you?

Are they telling you that it's not okay to feel sad? Are they telling you that true Christians don't take medication or seek help? Or are they open and honest with talking about the realities of living as cracked pots in a very broken world?

I remember, some years ago when I was deeply depressed, crying out to God, praying prayers similar to David's prayer in Psalm 6:3–6. David prayed: "My soul is in deep anguish. How long, LORD, how long? Turn, LORD, and deliver me; save me because of your unfailing love. … I am worn out from my groaning. All night long I flood my bed with weeping and drench my couch with tears" (NIV).

I recall praying that prayer during long nights of no sleep. I remember being so depressed, the only way I could get through is to set a TV next to my bed and watch the three original Star Wars movies on repeat. I was in a dark, dark place, and I didn't know how to deal with my feelings because I needed to submit myself to the culture of healing at my church.

It's time that we're open about our mental illness and struggle so that we can create safe cultures for people to get help.

Here are some simple ways we can create a culture that is a safe place to acknowledge and work through our mental health:

1. Be honest and open about your own mental health challenges.

2. Communicate clearly that your church is a place to run to rather than run away from when emotional healing is needed. Make it apparent that your church or organization is a place where it's okay not to be okay as long as you're on your way to change.

3. Be helpful by providing small groups at your church which are focused on biblical emotional healing.

4. Create an accessible referral list of trusted mental health professionals.

Mental health professionals state that the time when someone first shows the symptoms of mental illness to the time that they seek help is typically eight years. Think about the damage that can happen in a person's life in eight years! Let's work on our culture so that we can work on our mental health.

Tool 5: Chemistry

The fifth way to deal with how you are feeling is chemistry. Your biochemistry could be causing your condition, through no fault of your own! This is why it's important to get help, see a doctor, and get to the bottom of what is causing your feelings. It could be something that you are doing, but it also could be something that your body is doing against you.

Of course we pray for healing. God has the power to heal each and every one of us instantly, but remember the story of Paul. He had the thorn in his side, and instead of getting healing, he got grace (2 Corinthians 12:6–10). Sometimes meds, a good doctor, and a better understanding of your body is the lifeline that God will send you while He keeps working in the background.

Dr. Daniel Morehead says that we have to see our healing as a long-term war, and he believes that faith helps with this. He has stated scientific research that says that those who go to church and have faith are more likely to have good mental health. So keeping the faith, understanding that we are in a long-term battle, and getting to know our bodies are all keys to making the most of our chemistry and working through the way we feel.[8]

Tool 6: Choices

The sixth way to deal with how you feel involves your choices. Each of us has a choice. We can eat healthy and exercise or we can be lazy and eat fast food. We can think positive thoughts about ourselves or we can wallow in negative self-talk. We can choose healthy relationships or stay in the ones that make us feel angry and hurt. We can dive in with a church body, or we can fly solo. We can get lost in nature or in our smart phones.

Every day, we can choose how we live, and it's in these choices that God moves through the cracks of our lives. Let's make room for Him! Let's do our part by choosing what is good.

Tool 7: The Cross

All of these tools are possible because of the last tool that we have at our disposal: The cross of Christ.

Jesus had to be cracked so that you and I would have the opportunity to have a relationship with God. His power is made perfect in weakness (2 Corinthians 12:9), and we need Him if we're going to tackle these feelings head-on.

But we also need Him because sometimes the stuff going on isn't just in our heads. Sometimes, there are other forces at work. There are teachings in the Bible about how there are demonic forces all around that seek to steal, kill, and destroy (John 10:10). And you'd better believe they are coming at our mental health.

This is why we need the power of *the cross*. No demonic spirit has more power than *the cross*. No biochemistry has more power than *the cross*. If you feel trauma, past pain or failure, you can know that Jesus felt it on *the cross*. If you feel depression, you know that Jesus felt it on *the cross*. If you feel unlovable, you can know that Jesus felt that on *the cross*.

Colossians 2:14–15 says that "he canceled the record of the charges against us and took it away by nailing it to *the cross*. In this way, he disarmed the spiritual rulers and authorities. He shamed them publicly by his victory over them on *the cross*" (NLT, emphasis added). And then in Hebrews 12:2, we are told to fix "our eyes on Jesus, the pioneer and perfecter of faith. For the joy set before him he endured *the cross,* scorning its shame" (NIV, emphasis added). Jesus personally carried our sins to *the cross* so that we can be dead to these feelings and struggles and sins that plague us.

If you've never begun a personal relationship with God, the cross does you no good. That's why we need to stop the train for just a minute and take care of that. If you've never begun a relationship with Christ, it's simple to do. Just believe that when Jesus Christ died on the cross, He was doing so to pay the penalty for your sin.

Recently, I went to a nice restaurant and had lobster for my birthday. A dear friend paid the bill for me and everyone at our table. All we had to do was receive the gift. If you'd like to receive a love relationship with God right now, in this moment, just talk to Him through prayer. The words you pray are not as important as the attitude of your heart. Pray something like this:

> God, I know I've sinned and made significant mistakes. Right now, the best I know how, I choose to believe that Jesus Christ died on the cross to pay the penalty for my sin. Then He rose again to give me new life. Welcome into my life, God. Thank You for coming in.

The cross is the most powerful tool we have, and we have the opportunity to regularly claim the power of the cross for our healing.

God wants to help us navigate sadness, depression, anxiety, fear, hurt, pain, and so much more. He has given us tools to work with, from the cross to culture, from self-talk to our choices. It's time we choose to work through our feelings and allow God to come in and bring us one step closer to freedom in Him.

WORKBOOK

Chapter One Questions

Question: What are the *cracks* in your pot—areas of brokenness, suffering, trauma, or failure that keep you from living an abundant life in Christ? Describe what an abundant, whole, and healthy life would look like for you.

_____

_____

_____

_____

_____

_____

_____

_____

_____

_____

Question: Looking over these seven tools, which one(s) have you already been using effectively, and which ones do you need to focus on? For those tools that you need to start utilizing, who is someone you know who is already using that tool to bring healing and help to their life? What can you learn from observing this person? (If possible, ask them for advice on how to apply these tools to your own life.)

_____

_____

_____

_____

_____

_____

_____

_____

_____

_____

_____

Question: How have you experienced the power of the cross in your life? Do you see the cross as only relevant to salvation, or does it impact your daily life? How does Christ's victory over sin and death give you victory over the brokenness in your life, and how can you walk in that victory?

_____

_____

_____

_____

_____

_____

_____

_____

_____

_____

_____

_____

Action: If you do not already have a journal, acquire one to use for this study. Write down what you hope to learn and areas where you want to see healing. Then outline a plan for how you will begin to use or grow in your understanding of each of the seven tools at your disposal.

Chapter One Notes

_____

_____

_____

_____

_____

_____

_____

_____

_____

_____

_____

_____

_____

_____

_____

_____

_____

_____

_____

_____

_____

_____

CHAPTER TWO

Know Who Is at Fault

A few years ago, I met Mike and Jen. They're both Air Force Academy graduates, and it shows. They're smart and tough. They're strong-willed and determined. They have every quality that you look for in a solid leader.

When they came to me, Jen was experiencing substantial depression that was clouding her entire life. They explained to me that Jen grew up in a home in which her stepdad was a psychologist. At the time, he was into new age spirituality, and because of this, she received a spirit guide named Michael. The years went by. She met Mike, and they got married. Then Jen began to encounter what's called automatic writing.

Automatic writing is when something controls a person, making them write messages against their will. So Jen would find herself in a state of helplessness, scribbling message after message after message. Every single message she wrote was accusatory and hateful toward her Christ-following husband.

They came to me, at a loss for what to do. After hearing her story, I knew we needed to get rid of the spirit Michael that her stepfather had attached to her. You see, Michael was a demon. Since Michael is an archangel in the Bible, a lot of people think that spiritual experiences with someone named Michael are always good. Unfortunately, that's not true. He had seemed innocent enough over the years, but when Jen had an opportunity to move closer to the one true God, Michael went into action, doing everything he could to prevent that.

We prayed like crazy. We sent Michael packing and prayed some more. And by the grace of God, the cloud of depression is gone. Jen's life is forever changed.

There is a connection between mental health and the demonic. Some of it is intense, like what happened with Jen. But most of it is a lot less noticeable.

You see, we have a tendency as Christians to make sweeping generalizations. We say that *all* mental illness is demonic possession. When someone says that they're depressed, we advise them to toss the pill bottle and pray more. We tell them to "get right with Jesus."

But what we aren't willing to see are the small ways that the darkness has a hold on our lives. We refuse to acknowledge the delicacy of the situation, because reality is that yes, there is a spiritual world, and yes, there is physical health. And the way they work together to create the problems we deal with on a daily basis is intricate and difficult to navigate.

Most of us don't have a spirit guide named Michael. Most of us—whether we're diagnosed as mentally ill or not—are facing a much more subtle form of oppression. What we have is a corrupt thought life. We have selfish desires. We have jealousy, anger, and hate, and we think that because we aren't on a first-name basis with the demon on our back, we're okay.

But my friends, we are not okay.

Thinking About Your Thinking

We like to think that we're in control of our thoughts, but we're wrong. Dark images and thoughts creep in, and they jolt us awake. *"Where did that come from? Is that from me? Is that really what I think/ feel/ believe?"*

We give ourselves the third degree, trying to get to the bottom of how that thought got there, and what we don't consider are the spirits of this world. The beings that exist to pull us off track. We think that we're in control, but there is so much that we don't see.

Some years ago, I began to search for a connection between the spirit world and our thoughts and emotions. My seminary professor at the time, Dr. Roy Fish, spoke about these dark spiritual realities in a particular lecture that had a profound impact on many of us in his class. He spoke of things occurring that connect the spiritual world with our world in ways that we'd never imagined.

Later, I would hear Dr. David Allen, a Harvard and a Yale professor, say that he had experienced some of these manifestations. I also came across Dr. Richard Gallagher, a devout Catholic and board-certified psychiatrist and professor of clinical psychiatry at New York medical college, who helps Catholic priests in exorcisms. Dr Gallagher helps priests discern between mental illness and actual demon possession.[9]

There are a lot of smart people who openly recognize the connection between the demonic and our mental and emotional state, and the Bible backs this up.

In the account of the demon-possessed man in Mark 5, he is described like this:

> *He lived among the tombs. And no one could bind him anymore, not even with a chain, for he had often been bound with shackles and chains, but he wrenched the chains apart, and he broke the shackles in pieces. No one had the strength to subdue him. Night and day among the tombs and on the mountains he was always crying out and cutting himself with stones.*
>
> *—**Mark 5:3–5** (ESV)*

After Jesus healed the man from the demons, many came to see what had happened. It says they saw the man "sitting there, clothed and *in his right mind*" (Mark 5:15b ESV, emphasis added).

James 1:8 (NIV, emphasis added) says:

> *If any of you lacks wisdom, you should ask God, who gives generously to all without finding fault, and it will be given to you. But when you ask, you must believe and not doubt,*

*because the one who doubts is like a wave of the sea, blown and tossed by the wind. That person should not expect to receive anything from the Lord. **Such a person is double-minded and unstable in all they do.***

In Christ, we're supposed to have a single mindedness toward the kingdom of God, but our thoughts get confused and conflicted. It's like we're unstable emotionally and spiritually. Paul says, in 2 Corinthians 10:5, "We demolish arguments and every pretension that sets itself up against the knowledge of God, and we take captive every thought to make it obedient to Christ" (NIV).

So our thoughts affect our spiritual life *and* our emotional life. When this reality comes at us in ugly ways in the form of depression, anxiety, and suicidal thoughts, we beat ourselves up even more.

"If only I were more spiritual."

"If only I were stronger."

"If God really loved me, I wouldn't have to deal with this."

"If I were a good Christian, God would have taken care of this problem."

These thoughts cause us to cry out, *"Why is my life this way?"*

The Story of Job

The Bible tells us that one day when Satan was going back and forth across the earth looking for someone that he could harass, he happened upon Job. Job was a good, godly man, and Satan wanted to show that Job's faith would crack under a bit of pressure. He felt that God had protected Job and blessed him to such an extent that it was no wonder the man believed wholeheartedly in God. Satan said that if God took away Job's finances, his family, and his physical health, Job would curse God's face.

God gave Satan permission to test this theory, and so the devil got to work. He took out Job's finances, his family and his health, and the Bible tells us that Job was so miserable that he wished he'd never been born (Job 3).

Typically when Christians read the story of Job in this way, they read chapters 1 and 2, focusing on how Satan took everything away from a godly man. Then, they skip to the end, around chapter 42, where God restores Job's life and blesses him far beyond what he'd had.

The reason we skip the middle is because not much happens. Job spends dozens of chapters talking to his friends about his situation. But there's something in that middle that is incredibly significant.

A friend of Job named Eliphaz was a religious guy. In Job 4, Eliphaz had a spiritual experience that's very relevant to the topic of spiritual warfare and emotions.

A word was secretly brought to me, my ears caught a whisper of it. Amid disquieting dreams in the night, when deep sleep falls on people, fear and trembling seized me and made all my bones shake. A spirit glided past my face, and the hair on my body stood on end. It stopped, but I could not tell what it was. A form stood before my eyes, and I heard a hushed voice....

—*Job 4:12–16(NIV)*

This spirit that came by Eliphaz was making subtle accusations toward Job. It was saying things that were mostly true, but it would tweak the truth just enough to cause Eliphaz to question Job's character.

That is the way demons work. They never give you a bold-faced lie, but they'll give you a half-truth. They'll twist the meaning just enough to get you to respond. Then they tweak it a bit more and before you know it, you've fallen into their trap. You believe all kinds of things that you would normally be able to brush off. They are masters at deception, and all of a sudden, you're on the side of the road with smoke pouring out of your soul. This is why a regular spiritual tune-up, as I mentioned in the introduction, is so important.

So this passage was Eliphaz's spiritual experience with a demon. This demon began to influence him and his friends. He caused them to bring accusations toward Job, claiming that the horrible things that were happening had to be coming from a dark secret in Job's life! If only he would pray more, be better, and get right with God!

Well-meaning Christians do this all the time. They try to correlate your suffering to your sin, but they miss the fact that there is a spiritual realm always at work against us!

That was the case in Job's story. His own friends were instruments of Satan, used to accuse Job during the time of his life that he needed encouragement the most from his friends. People think they're doing the Lord's work, speaking truth into your life. But sometimes they're actually doing the work of Satan.

It's not only other people that make these accusations. We make them, too. Demons trick us into pointing the finger at anybody but them.

Accusing Ourselves

Dealing with sin in our lives should be an ongoing thing. It should involve digging deep and removing whatever it is that's causing us to stumble. When the Holy Spirit taps our spirit and says, *"Hey, this is something that needs to change,"* we need to listen. We need to act.

But what we don't want is for our own shortcomings and fallenness to crush our spirit to such an extent that we can't even receive the healing power of the cross.

The cross bridges the gap between our sin and God's glory. We cannot lose sight of that!

No demon is more powerful than the cross. No accusing thought is more powerful than the cross. No damaged biochemistry is more powerful than the cross. No trauma or past failure is more powerful than the cross. No shame in your life over something you did wrong is more powerful than the cross.

If you feel unlovable, if that demon on your back has convinced you that you've messed up too much to enter into God's love, then I am here to tell you that's a lie. Nothing will separate us from His love.

Everything you feel ashamed or guilty about, He took

that upon himself on the cross. First Peter 2:24 says, "He personally carried our sins in his body on the cross so that we can be dead to sin and live for what is right. By his wounds you are healed" (NLT).

But sometimes this truth is hard to receive. There may be a voice in your head saying, *"How can you be a church volunteer after all the stuff you've done?"* That voice isn't from the Holy Spirit.

Or there may be something inside you saying, *"You act like you're trying to walk with God, but you looked at porn a few nights ago! There's no hope for you; you're a pervert. God doesn't love you."* That voice isn't from the Holy Spirit.

As a spouse, you might be hearing, *"You're not a good husband or wife! If you made more money, if you looked better, if you provided more, then you'd be worthy of love!"* That voice isn't from the Holy Spirit.

As an employee or student, you may be dealing with a voice that tells you, if only you were smarter, better, or more qualified, then you'd be worthy. But that voice isn't coming from the Holy Spirit.

These accusations only tear us down. Yes, we have things we need to work on, but by the grace of God, we are forgiven and loved. Romans 8:1 says that "there is now no condemnation for those who are in Christ Jesus" (NIV).

Accusing Other People

Sometimes when we don't know how to deal with a situation, or when we don't want to take ownership of our role in it, we blame others. And while there are times that those accusations are valid, more often than not, they only divide people. In this way, the devil uses our blame and accusations against us.

There is no need to point the finger unless you're going to be part of the solution. The moment we accuse someone just to make ourselves look good or feel better, then we're doing it from the wrong spirit, and the devil is celebrating.

Before you accuse, check your heart. Pray and ask God to remove the desire to needlessly accuse. Confess the times you've fallen short in this area, and choose to change. Choose to believe the best about others and then command the evil spirit tempting you to accuse to depart.

Accusing God

Lastly—and this is a big one—the devil loves it when we blame God. It's easy to do. Suffering or loss happens, and your first thought is to ask God why? Why didn't He come through? Why did He allow it?

Job's friends did it. The book of Job is clear that it was Satan bringing about the suffering, yet Job's friends didn't see it that way. They blamed God.

How often do we blame God, ourselves, or others for things that the devil has orchestrated? And on the flip side, how often do we over-spiritualize what's happening and dump it all on Satan when there is so much more going on with genetics, body chemistry, and more?

We will always have a desire to place blame, but God calls us to trust Him. Let's recognize the role the devil plays *and* the role that we play. Let's enter into this with clear minds, no agendas. And let's know that God is good. He has always been good. And only He has our best interests at heart. So let's trust and follow Him.

Now that you're choosing to trust Him, the Holy Spirit can speak to you about accusing other people. Do any names come to mind? If so, put the name of the accused in the appropriate blank and pray the following prayer out loud.

> Heavenly Father, in Jesus' name, I confess that I've unnecessarily accused _____. I choose to change. I will no longer accuse _____. I choose to believe the best about others. In Jesus' name, I command the accusing spirit to go now. Holy Spirit, please fill me and speak truth to my mind.

If you've struggled with accusing yourself, pray the following prayer out loud.

> Heavenly Father, in Jesus' name, I confess that I've unnecessarily accused myself. I choose to change. I will no longer accuse myself. I choose to embrace my identity in Christ. In Jesus' name, I command the accusing spirit to go now. Holy Spirit, please fill me and speak truth to my mind.

If you've struggled with blaming or accusing God, pray the following prayer out loud.

Heavenly Father, in Jesus' name, I confess that I've accused You of doing me wrong. I choose to change. I will no longer accuse You, God. I know You are good. In Jesus' name, I command the accusing spirit to go now. Holy Spirit, please fill me and speak truth to my mind.

Close your eyes and listen for a word, picture, or thought from the Spirit.

WORKBOOK

Chapter Two Questions

Question: Do you tend to over-spiritualize or under-spiritualize your problems? That is, do you consider the possibility of demonic influence as well as normal physical and emotional factors, or do you tend to focus entirely on one to the exclusion of the other?

_____

_____

_____

_____

_____

_____

_____

_____

_____

_____

Question: Who are some people from your past or present that you tend to blame for your problems? Have you thought or verbalized accusations against them? How can you honestly acknowledge their wrong while also taking responsibility for your own wellbeing and health?

_____

_____

_____

_____

_____

_____

_____

_____

_____

_____

_____

_____

Question: Describe a time when you blamed God. Looking back, can you see now how He was at work in that situation? How did He demonstrate His goodness even in the midst of your suffering? What have you learned about trusting Him because of the difficulty that you went through?

_____

_____

_____

_____

_____

_____

_____

_____

_____

_____

_____

_____

_____

Action: Read Revelation 12:10. What is Satan called in this verse? What are some of the accusations that you "hear" against yourself on a regular basis? For each, write down and memorize a Scripture that tells the truth of how God sees you and who He is in your life.

Chapter Two Notes

_____

_____

_____

_____

_____

_____

_____

_____

_____

_____

_____

_____

_____

_____

_____

_____

_____

_____

_____

_____

_____

_____

_____

_____

CHAPTER THREE

Deal with Bitterness

When we talk about emotional health and the demonic, we're not saying that everybody who has any type of emotional health issue is demon-possessed and requires an exorcism. We're not saying that if you have been prescribed meds, you should throw them away and pray more. Certainly, there are people who overmedicate, and certainly, we would all be better off if we prayed more.

What we're doing is acknowledging that there is a connection between our emotional wellbeing and the demonic.

The great Oxford scholar and author C. S. Lewis said,

"There are two equal and opposite errors into which our race can fall about the devils. One is to disbelieve in their existence. The other is to believe, and to feel an excessive and unhealthy interest in them."[10]

In other words, the way we think—the things we believe and disbelieve, the things that capture our interest—matter very much. The mind is powerful. And that's why we've got to think about our thinking.

I have a saying that "thinking about your thinking is not overthinking." We need to be aware of what's going on in our minds, and we've got to adjust our thoughts.

This is the best way to fend off those dark forces that seep into our lives and wreak havoc, but before we dive in, let's make some important declarations. If you're comfortable, put your hand out in a position to receive from the Holy Spirit of God. I want you to say these declarations out loud:

- God is for me, not against me.
- God has loving motives for me.
- I'm no longer a victim, but a conqueror.
- I receive healing in the deepest parts of my soul today.
- I receive spiritual freedom today.
- Jesus is awesome.

Let's dive in and begin the hard work of thinking about our thinking.

Symptoms of a Greater Problem

Years ago, I was going through a fairly significant depression. During that time, I went through a lot of extensive counseling and recovery processes on the outer layers of my soul. I found that my depression was just a symptom of something deeper that was going on. The lust I was struggling with was also a symptom.

Most of the time, a lot of our outward dysfunctional behaviors are really just symptoms of a much deeper issue. My depression seemed like my ultimate foe, but it was really caused by something much greater. For me, it was a deep-rooted bitterness in my heart.

I've read the Bible, and I know that you're supposed to forgive people. I'd even said the words of forgiveness, but for some reason, they didn't take. I had forgiven on the surface level, but the next layer down held bitterness and unforgiveness.

I could tell you all the ways that significant people in my life disappointed me, wounded me, and hurt me. I could tell you why I was justified in my hurt and anger toward them. I'm sure you would feel sorry for me if you knew all the ways I've been hurt.

The reason I don't write in this book about the most significant ways I've been hurt is that a part of my own forgiveness journey is to never publicly dishonor those who have hurt me. I've worked through those hurts with several qualified therapists, who know every detail of how I've been hurt and by whom.

Now, when I realize that I'm holding onto unforgiveness, I go to that person, or to a trusted mentor, and I talk about the ways I've been wounded. This gets it out in the open. It forces me to deal with what's going on.

And then what I found was that there was a third layer. A *core* layer. Under bitterness and unforgiveness was a theological issue—it's always a theological issue. It was something that I had believed about God.

In my heart, I believed that God wouldn't exert His power to change my heart. I believed that if I dared to forgive, God still wouldn't give me healing from the depression.

And you know what that was? That was me questioning God's motives and His love for me.

During that time, I was going to a Christian psychiatrist. He prescribed me some antidepressants, but they didn't work. So instead, I chose to lean into all of the pain of what I was going through in the counseling recovery process. I dealt with that deep theological issue I was struggling with, and I saw God come through for me.

And that's what I want for you.

Your sadness, your depression, your anxiety, your

pain—these are symptoms. They point to a much deeper problem that is rooted in an incorrect view of, and relationship with, God.

Grace and Justice

While we are all dealing with many different issues, unforgiveness is one of the big ones. A significant number of us have bitterness or unforgiveness issues toward our parents, mentors, and loved ones. As I write this, I'm painfully aware that some of you have been cheated on by a spouse, lied to, sexually abused by someone you trusted, or violently beaten. In no way am I minimizing what you've endured.

As you read the following story, think about the people who have hurt you the most.

Then Peter came to Jesus and asked, "Lord, how many times shall I forgive my brother or sister who sins against me? Up to seven times?"

Jesus answered, "I tell you, not seven times, but seventy-seven times.

"Therefore, the kingdom of heaven is like a king who wanted to settle accounts with his servants. As he began the settlement, a man who owed him ten thousand bags of gold was brought to him. Since he was not able to pay, the master ordered that he and his wife and his children and all that he had be sold to repay the debt.

"At this the servant fell on his knees before him. 'Be patient with me,' he begged, 'and I will pay back everything.' The servant's master took pity on him, canceled the debt and let him go.

"But when that servant went out, he found one of his fellow servants who owed him a hundred silver coins. He grabbed him and began to choke him. 'Pay back what you owe me!' he demanded.

"His fellow servant fell to his knees and begged him, 'Be patient with me, and I will pay it back.'

"But he refused. Instead, he went off and had the man thrown into prison until he could pay the debt. When the other servants saw what had happened, they were outraged and went and told their master everything that had happened.

"Then the master called the servant in. 'You wicked servant,' he said, 'I canceled all that debt of yours because you begged me to. Shouldn't you have had mercy on your fellow servant just as I had on you?' In anger his master handed him over to the jailers to be tortured, until he should pay back all he owed.

"This is how my heavenly Father will treat each of you unless you forgive your brother or sister from your heart."
—Matthew 18:21–35(NIV)

In my personal story, bitterness and unforgiveness in my heart handed me over to the torture of depression and other dysfunctional behaviors that I did not want in my life. It was as if God were saying, "Since you won't turn to Me and trust in Me, then I will turn you over to your own demise."

"How can God be so cruel?" you're probably wondering. Two significant parts of God are His grace and His justice. When God gets angry, it is for good reason. He is angered because of injustice and wrongdoing.

Some people don't truly want the real God. They want a snuggle-bunny, care-bear God. They want a sweet, happy, positive-thinking kind of guy who never gets mad about sin.

But thinking about your thinking doesn't mean glossing over your own sin. When you come to God, humble yourself to Him, repent or turn from your sin, and start to obey Him, you'll find Him waiting with open arms. You'll find that loving, caring Father. This side of Him is what He intended for you to experience, but we get in the way. Injustice happens. We doubt His goodness. We make bad choices. We turn away from Him, and He has to respond.

But the key thing to remember is that He always forgives.

When Peter asked Jesus about forgiveness in the Matthew passage, he thought he knew the answer. Peter knew Jesus to be a forgiving guy, and so Peter suggested that we forgive seven times—that's many more times than the common Jewish practice in that day of forgiving someone three times. So Peter had to have felt pretty good about his answer. But Jesus one-upped him.

"Seventy-seven times" was Jesus' way of saying, "Always forgive. No matter what."

Forgiveness should be infinite.

Then Jesus gave the illustration of the different servants. One owed the equivalent of eleven years of taxes for *four* provinces. That's like owing the U. S. national debt! When he fell to his knees, begging his debtor for forgiveness, the king gave it gladly. He set the man free.

But that very man whose debt had just been forgiven turned around and threw his own servant in jail for failing to pay his much-smaller debt.

When the king found out about this, he handed the

servant he had forgiven over to the jailers. God has no patience for people who accept forgiveness from Him but then refuse it to others. I agree with author Anne Lamott's assessment: "Not forgiving is like drinking rat poison and then waiting for the rat to die."[11]

Forgiveness Is a Choice

I'm convinced that forgiveness is one of the big issues plaguing us today, not because of how bad we are, but because of how good we are. We think that it's okay to withhold forgiveness because we've done a bunch of other good things that will make up for it. We think of our actions piling up on a judgment scale. The good actions, far outweighing the bad. And so we continue to hold onto bitterness.

Paul wrote in his letter to the Romans that all have sinned and fallen short of God's glory (Romans 3:23). Yes, even if you've lived a good life, you've fallen short. Even if you made straight A's in school, served the homeless, volunteered at church, and recycled your trash. you've still fallen short. Some people's goodness blinds them from admitting their need for God and forgiveness from Him. If a person doesn't recognize their need for God's forgiveness, they'll never recognize their need to forgive other people.

Forgiveness will never be appealing. It will never be fun or exciting. It's hard, because it's a choice we have to make day after day after day. I used to think that forgiveness was a one-time event. Then I'd get frustrated when the hurtful, unforgiving feelings resurfaced. Then it dawned on me that in Jesus' model prayer, known as the Lord's Prayer, He is giving us a prayer to pray daily, which includes, "Forgive us our debts, as we also have forgiven our debtors" (Matthew 6:12 ESV). Forgiveness is a daily act of faith.

This may be the first time you've considered this. Or if you're like me, you've read the Scriptures, you know what God says about forgiveness, and yet here you are. Holding onto that resentment and bitterness against someone else.

But all of us are that servant standing before God. We owe a debt. Some of us think that we've done enough to repay that debt, but the reality of the teaching of the Bible is that all have sinned and fall short of the glory of God. All of us. That includes Mother Theresa, Billy Graham, your pastor, your mentor, me, and you. We have fallen short (Romans 3:23). That's what sin literally means. We've missed the mark, and God is too perfect and pure to allow those who have missed the mark into His kingdom.

That's why He offers forgiveness. He wipes out your biggest debt. And He expects you to do the same for others.

Bitterness, resentment, holding onto the past will make way for demonic forces in your life. Choose forgiveness daily. Choose freedom. And watch as those layers of pain and anxiety fall away.

Perhaps it would be helpful for you to pray a prayer of forgiveness right now. I know this is going to be hard for you because of the pain you feel over how badly you were hurt. You can do this! Just read over this prayer, and insert the name of the person who hurt you and the offense in the appropriate blanks below. Then speak this prayer out loud.

> Heavenly Father, in the name of Jesus, I choose to forgive _____ for _____. I now ask You to forgive me for all the resentment, bitterness, and judgment I have had toward them. I cancel all of Satan's power and authority over me in this area, because God has forgiven me and I have forgiven _____.

WORKBOOK

Chapter Three Questions

Question: Is there an underlying issue of bitterness/ unforgiveness in your life? Who was your offender, and how did this person wrong you? Why do you feel justified in refusing forgiveness? What symptoms of unforgiveness have shown up in your life?

_____

_____

_____

_____

_____

_____

_____

_____

_____

Question: How have you experienced God's forgiveness for your own sins? Do you regularly thank Him for His forgiveness? Do you see it as His grace or as something you deserve?

_____

_____

_____

_____

_____

_____

_____

_____

_____

_____

_____

Question: Who is God calling you to forgive? Are you taking steps of obedience or disobedience? What can you do when _feelings_ of bitterness arise despite the _choice_ you have made to forgive?

_____

_____

_____

_____

_____

_____

_____

_____

_____

_____

_____

_____

Action: Commit to spending the next several days thinking about your thinking. Jot down lists of thoughts that you regularly have about yourself, God, and others. Then examine these thoughts in light of Scripture. To what deeper issues do they point? What changes do you need to make in your thought patterns and motivations?

Chapter Three Notes

CHAPTER FOUR

Deal with Fear

There's an article in *Scientific American* about a man named Tom who witnessed an accident.[12] A cyclist was biking on a road when the cyclist was run over by a Camaro. In the chaos of the event, the cyclist ended up stuck underneath the car.

Tom didn't wait to act. He went over to the Camaro and lifted it high enough for another bystander to pull the cyclist to safety. Now if you see pictures of Tom in the article, you'll see that Tom is a big guy. He's strong. But a stock Camaro is three thousand pounds, and last I checked, the world-record dead lift is a little over one thousand pounds.

Something happened that day that caused Tom to channel superhuman strength. According to the article, that *something* was the body's fear response.

When we find ourselves under intense pressure, fear unleashes reserves of energy that normally remain inaccessible. We become in effect, superhuman. Fear gives us superhuman awareness and abilities. It makes us more alert, more energized, more anxious. While good fear empowers us to act, there is also a bad form of fear that paralyzes us, rendering us immobile.

This bad fear is controlled by our thoughts, and it's time we take back control.

Power of Fear

Back in the '90s, Art Mathias was suffering from a disease called peripheral neuropathy. It caused him to be allergic to most foods; there was hardly anything that he could eat without having some type of a reaction. His doctors told him he was certain to die within two years.

Art continued to follow God and try to serve Him as he suffered, but his body just wouldn't cooperate. His mind was also defeated. How do you keep the faith when you have a death sentence hanging over you?

In his book *Biblical Foundations for Freedom*,[13] Art shares that he got on the phone with his sister, who talked to him about a unique tool that she called "praying-through." It was an extensive process, in which she met with people and dealt with unforgiveness issues, fear issues, and more. She prayed through those issues, sometimes spending much of her time in deep, concerted prayer. She noticed things began to change. And eventually, a physical condition that had slowed her down was healed. She suggested Art give it a try.

Though he was skeptical, he submitted himself to the process of working through and praying through everything that was in his life. Implementing a fearless moral inventory, he worked on forgiveness issues and fears that were rooted deep within.

And he was healed. The peripheral neuropathy—gone.

People couldn't believe it. So many came to him, asking what he had done to get healing, that he went to school, got a doctorate in counseling, and opened Wellspring Ministries. To this day, Wellspring helps people deal with their significant fear issues, and they're getting healed as a result.

Now, I'm not saying that every time we pray for something, someone's going to get healed. While God is absolutely in the healing business, He's not a genie granting wishes. We will all die at some point, Art included! But I think we need to take seriously the connection between fear and physical health.

Harvard Medical School tells us that anxiety and fear can contribute to painful physical conditions.[14] Could it be that a lot of us are dealing with physical ailments when healing is available to us through conquering our fears? Could it be that if we root fear out of our hearts, we may see better health and immune systems? Could this be yet another area where the demonic is winning the war over our thoughts and lives?

Calling Out to God

In Psalm 3:2–8 (NIV), David prays:

LORD, how many are my foes! How many rise up against me! Many are saying of me, "God will not deliver him."

But you, LORD, are a shield around me, my glory, the One who lifts my head high. I call out to the LORD, and he answers me from his holy mountain.

I lie down and sleep; I wake again, because the LORD sustains me. I will not fear though tens of thousands assail me on every side.

Arise, LORD! Deliver me, my God! Strike all my enemies on the jaw; break the teeth of the wicked.

From the LORD comes deliverance. May your blessing be on your people.

I love the way David prays. He's raw and honest. He's real. He doesn't clean things up, trying to make himself look a certain way. He's vulnerable, and in this prayer, he boldly asks God to kick his enemies in the teeth (Psalm 3:7)!

People deal with and process their fears and negative emotions in different ways. In recovery, we say that some people are stuffers. They just stuff it all down and never deal with it at all. It's too painful, so they never talk about it. The problem with this is that stuffers eventually blow up.

Some people are venters. They get it all out. They'll tell anybody *all* their emotions to the point of overload.

The problem with venters is that such a hyper-focus on their problems breeds an environment of constant negativity.

David chooses a third way, a whole different method. He unloads his feelings, but he does this strategically. He unloads on someone who can actually help. He calls to God as he processes his fears, and as he does this, he reminds himself of the support and love and protection he has in God. And this doesn't end in Psalm 3. A majority of the book of Psalms consists of David's prayers, where he gets real with God and seeks calming for his fears.

Common Fears

What is it that you fear the most? What keeps you up at night or makes you sweat?

Some are afraid of intimacy. They're afraid of growing close in relationships, and for some, this fear is rooted in a fear of rejection. They've been rejected before, they've been hurt before, and so they're not letting anyone in to see the real them.

Some are afraid of commitment. You see this many times in divorcees. They refuse to get married again because their first marriage was so painful.

You also see this in church. People who have been hurt by church leaders or spiritual mentors are afraid to connect to a church body. So they stay on the fringe.

Some are afraid of being single. These people lower their standards for a romantic partner, because they're afraid of being alone. They're afraid that this may be their last chance at a relationship, and so you end up with couples who aren't matched up on the spiritual side. One is fully committed to following Christ, and the other is not. This causes a flood of problems when marriage and kids come along.

There's a fear of failure. Some people fear failure so much that they spend all their time at the office working. They miss out on relationships and experiences that God has for them.

Some fear missing out on life. We call this FOMO (fear of missing out). These folks look at their social media, Instagram, and Snapchat, and they see how everyone else's lives look so perfect. They see a party that they weren't invited to, or an event that they missed out on, and they get depressed. They assume that everyone else is having a wonderful life while they are not. They're afraid of not having what others have.

There's a fear of violence. School shootings and violent crimes are all over the news, and fear sets in. Many houses of worship are having to increase security because of church shootings. Many purchase guns for home protection. While safeguards are wise, fear goes a step further. It debilitates us and keeps us from living normal lives. Those under fear's control don't go to school or church due to their fear. We need not live under fear's control.

Calling-Out God

It's important to understand the context of Psalm 3. David was being hunted down by his rogue son, Absalom. In Star Wars terms, I think of Absalom as the Kylo Ren of the Bible. Absalom was evil, hunting down his dad with a group of soldiers to try to kill him so that he, Absalom, could claim sole right to his father's throne.

So, when David wrote about thousands of people coming after him (Psalm 3:6), he wasn't exaggerating. An army was coming for him. And when he wrote, "Many are saying of me, 'God will not deliver him'" (Psalm 3:2), he was referring to how the people were saying that God had abandoned David just like he'd abandoned Saul. Saul was king before David. He was manipulative and controlling. He was filled with fear, and he disobeyed orders from God. That is why God rejected him.

The people had every reason to believe that David would follow in Saul's footsteps. Look at David's track record. Here was a guy who had committed adultery with Bathsheba (2 Samuel 11:1–13). Then, he murdered Bathsheba's husband, Uriah the Hittite, to cover up his wrongdoing (2 Samuel 11:14–27). David did many awful things in his life. *"Is this really the type of person that God wants as king?"*

But as Psalm 3 shows, David still had faith. He believed God would stay with him, even though he had to be terrified of what was ahead, and he boldly declared his faith. He called out God.

David called out God's protective nature, the "shield" (Psalm 3:3). A shield is only useful when you're facing forward. Turn around to flee, and you're exposed. The shield can't help you. God is our shield, our protector as we boldly face whatever is in our path. This is the opposite of fear!

In Ephesians 6:10–20, Paul talked about the armor of

God. He wrote about taking up the shield of faith (v. 16). Having *faith* in God rather than *fear* of the enemy. If you have faith, you have courage to move into and through your problems. You can't go around your fear. You can't run from your fear. You have to face it head-on and go towards the battle. This is how you conquer fear.

For some of us, taking up the shield means having to face the fear of a tough conversation to mend fences. For some it means taking the step to start that business God has placed on your heart. It means moving toward the vision He gave you. It means tackling that problem area that you're afraid of facing. It means working through past hurts.

Fear manifests itself in so many ways, but the only way to defeat it is to move through it by holding onto faith in God's promises.

Calling Out Others

David didn't stop at calling out God. He called out other people, too. He prayed, "May your blessing be on your people" (Psalm 3:8 NIV). Even in his distress and fear, David didn't lose his heart for others. He loved his people, and he was willing to fight his own son if it meant preventing his country from being ruled by a monster.

Even in our fear, we can still shepherd and look out for others. First John 4:18 says that "there is no fear in love, but perfect love drives out fear" (NIV). It's hard to dwell in fear when you're focused on loving others, when you're serving others, welcoming others, helping others. This is the reason why parents will put themselves in harm's way for their children. It's the power of love! David knew this, and he channeled his love to help him overcome his fear. He chose this instead of choosing hate.

Calling Out Your Glory

Last, David called out his glory. He prayed, "But you, LORD, are a shield around me, my glory, the One who lifts my head high" (Psalm 3:3 NIV).

At this point in his life, David had lost whatever he could have considered his glory or his identity. He was no longer popular. People weren't singing songs about him anymore. He had lost his wealth. He had lost his power. His own son had turned on him. David had lost everything.

We all have that *one thing* we fear losing the most. Maybe it's wealth, health, popularity, your home, your family, your job. I have heard it said, "Fear is the response of the human heart when its *one thing* is threatened."

I remember when my "glory" was my ministry. It was my *one thing* that I held onto, that I feared losing the most. It wasn't until I was forced to spend some years out of the ministry that I found my true identity, my true glory, as a servant of God. I realized I didn't have to be *Pastor Doug.* I could just be Doug, follower of Christ.

I want you to have the same realization that I had and that David had. I want you to understand that even if you lose the things that mean the most to you, you still have *everything.*

David wasn't shaken, because he knew God was with him. He knew this, because he saw his prayers being answered: "I call out to the LORD and he answers me from his Holy mountain" (Psalm 3:4 NIV).

At the end of the day, that's all we need. A God who hears us and who answers. A God who is with us even when we've lost everything we hold dear.

Faith Over Fear

Psalm 3 shows us that David clung to God's faithfulness because he knew that God can be trusted. He maintained his love for people, and he confirmed that God was his glory. This is how David navigated one of the most fearful times of his life. He had every reason to cower and break, but he stayed strong.

This is possible for us, too. While fear is one of the enemy's primary strategies to get in our heads and mess with our faith, we have tools to combat it. We can do what David did. We can call on the name of the Lord, call on His glory, love others, and keep our focus on the eternal, not the temporary.

Try this today with whatever you're facing. Whatever fear you have, pray your own version of Psalm 3 over and over and let God do His mighty work of cleansing your mind of the fear that is gripping it.

In fact, go ahead and talk to God right now. Quiet your mind and pray the following prayers.

Jesus, I ask You to bring to mind memories from my past that brought fear into my heart.

Take a moment to listen.

Dear Heavenly Father, I confess that I have allowed fear to control me. I renounce the spirit of *fear*. I choose to live by faith, *not* fear. In Jesus' name and by His blood, I cancel Satan's authority over me from the *fear*. In Jesus' name, I command *fear* to leave me now with all its works and effects. Holy Spirit, I invite You to fill me and heal me from the deepest roots of *fear*. Holy Spirit, please give me a word, picture, or thought about my life now.

Take a moment to listen. Now make these truth declarations out loud.

God has not given me a spirit of fear. (2 Timothy 1:7)

I have power, love, and discipline. (2 Timothy 1:7)

I'm no longer a victim but a conqueror. (Romans 8:37)

I'm filled with faith, not fear. (Mark 4:40)

I'm no longer a slave to fear. (Galatians 4:7)

WORKBOOK

Chapter Four Questions

Question: What effects have fear and anxiety had on your physical and mental health? How have they impacted your relationships? How have they influenced your decisions?

_____

_____

_____

_____

_____

_____

_____

_____

_____

_____

_____

_____

Question: Are you more prone to stuffing your feelings or venting them? What are some potential negative consequences of either extreme? How, practically, can you entrust your fears and emotions to the Lord? What are some other potential safe places or safe people that can help you share your worries, fears, and hurts in an appropriate and healing manner?

_____

_____

_____

_____

_____

_____

_____

_____

_____

_____

_____

Question: Who do you love so much that you would face your greatest fears in order to help them? How does fear naturally damage relationships, and how can you allow love to overcome your specific fears and heal those relationships?

_____

_____

_____

_____

_____

_____

_____

_____

_____

_____

_____

_____

Action: Make a list of your fears and worries. What is your *one thing* you fear losing more than anything else? Call out who God is over each item on your list. Write down a name, attribute, or promise of God that speaks directly to His power over the situation. Evaluate your fears in light of what is eternal and God's promise to always be with you.

Chapter Four Notes

_____

_____

_____

_____

_____

_____

_____

_____

_____

_____

_____

_____

_____

_____

_____

_____

_____

_____

_____

_____

_____

_____

_____

CHAPTER FIVE

Deal with Rejection

Remember the old Nirvana song, "I Hate Myself and Wanna Die?"[15] That's a real pick-me-up. Or how about that Kelly Clarkson song, "I Hate Myself for Losing You"?[16] Or when Lee Ann Womack sang, "I may hate myself in the morning, but I'm going to love you to-night"?[17]

Really think about those words. We live in a culture of self-hate and self-rejection. And you know what? This comes straight from the demonic. Evil spirits have infiltrated our thinking, convincing us that we are inadequate.

The only cure for thoughts of rejection is what we call "salvation identification."

Indicators of Self-Rejection

"Well, I don't struggle with that!" You may be thinking this right now, but let me walk you through what self-rejection and self-negativity look like.

They look like self-pity. This is someone who is always feeling sorry for himself, who is always a victim to what happened years ago.

They look like self-humiliation. This is someone who thrives on self-deprecating humor. Don't get me wrong: it's okay to feel comfortable enough with ourselves to poke a little fun and not take life too seriously. But when that is the primary way we get people to like us and accept us—when it becomes part of who we are—it's a symptom of self-rejection.

Self-rejection and self-negativity look like someone who is self-focused. This is someone who demands attention and for everything to be about them. They manipulate situations to bring the spotlight back on themselves. I saw this firsthand when I went to visit a friend who was in the hospital. His wife struggled with this form of self-rejection. She maneuvered the conversation to be about her and how the whole scenario affected *her* life. During my entire visit, she never said one word about how her husband might feel about his diagnosis.

Sometimes self-rejection looks like competition and comparison. It's a slippery slope to compare ourselves to other people. You'll always find someone who's better than you, more popular than you, more successful. I find this with a lot with pastors. Pastors are always comparing themselves to one another. They compare church size and growth. They compare social media reach and the health of their congregations. But God doesn't always use numbers of "likes" and "fans" to indicate success.

Self-rejection can look like people who talk too much or talk too little. These people are either constantly trying to sell their goods or are afraid that if they speak up, what they say will be rejected.

Self-rejection can look like religious legalism. These people believe that if they follow all the rules perfectly, then they're okay. They're accepted. The more stringent the rules, the better! They view God as an all-powerful judge who is waiting for them to mess up. But really, it is their own inability to accept imperfections that is causing this behavior.

Self-rejection can look like bodily abuse. This can manifest in overeating, undereating, and unhealthy sexual practices. It can look like cutters and self-mutilators. But at its core are people who have rejected themselves, so they believe they must punish themselves.

All You Need Is Love

In American culture, we're taught from an early age to love ourselves, but clearly many of us have failed to learn that lesson. So many of us have rejected ourselves for one reason or another. We just don't like ourselves very much, and this self-hate is a playground for demonic activity.

So I'd like to introduce a new concept. How about

instead of figuring out how to love ourselves, we figure out how to love God?

In Matthew 22, God tells us how He views us. People were asking Jesus, "What's the greatest command?" They were trying to trick him to see if he upheld the law of Moses. But Jesus replied that you must "'love the Lord your God with all your heart and with all your soul and with all your mind.' This is the first and greatest commandment. And the second is like it: 'Love your neighbor as yourself'" (Matthew 22:37–39 NIV).

This passage is often unpacked to mean that you can't love your neighbor unless you appropriately love yourself, but that's only part of the equation. The part that many leave out is the call to love God.

Loving yourself and loving others are both incomplete without first loving God.

A lot of people come to church to get something from God. They're going through a problem, or they need provision, so they decide it's time to get serious about church. But going to God and approaching Him that way doesn't always work. The first step isn't moving toward God so that we can get something in return. The first step should be to learn to love God.

When you love God, you get more of God. You find all you need, *including* everything you need to deal with your own self-rejection. And those parts of you that you don't love? God fills those when you turn to Him and love Him.

Think about your friends. The reason you like your friends is because you've spent time with them. You've gotten to know them, and you've poured into those relationships. You give and give, and then your friends give in return. That's true relationship.

It works the same way with God. Spend time with Him, invest in relationship with Him, and you will find just how caring and loyal and giving of a friend He can be.

When you get to know God, you'll get to know His brilliance, His holiness, His love. Instead of using Him because He's so grand, you'll want to submit your life to Him, to love Him, to worship Him, to lean into Him. You'll quickly get over self-rejection when you lean into the greatness, grandeur, and glory of God. His perfection influences us, and soon we see ourselves the way that He sees us. Not as rejected, but as accepted. As loved. As worthy.

The Hebrew creation story is like a poem. It has a rhythm and a cadence to it. The poem says God created light and darkness and it was good. He created sky and water, and it was good. He created plants and trees; it was good. He created fish and animals; it was good. Then, God created humans. Genesis 1:31 says, "God saw all that he made, and it was very good" (NIV).

Very good. Humanity is the greatest of God's creation.

Fast forward to David in Psalm 139:14. David wrote, "Thank you for making me so wonderfully complex! Your workmanship is marvelous—how well I know it" (NLT). David saw himself the way God sees us. But if you keep reading through Scripture, you'll find that Isaiah and the Jewish people oftentimes felt rejected by God. They felt they had sinned too much or that God wasn't as present as He had once been. Isaiah 49:14–16 touches on this. "The LORD has deserted us; the LORD has forgotten us"

(v. 14 NLT).

But just as self-rejection started to creep in, Isaiah was reminded of how God sees him. He went on to write, "Never! Can a mother forget her nursing child? Can she feel no love for a child she has borne? But even if that were possible, I would not forget you! See, I have written your name on the palms of my hands" (v. 15–16 NLT). God has written your name on the palms of His hands! It's like God has a tattoo of your name on the palm of His hand! You are truly special to Him.

If you feel like you've gone too far from God, He reaches out to you. You are His greatest accomplishment, and there is nothing you can do to move away from His love. You are accepted—no matter what.

God's Movie

Pastor and author Louie Giglio once said that if life is a movie, God should be the star.[18] When I think about this, it reminds me of one of my longtime fantasies. I imagine that the Avengers producer, Kevin Feige, is in town for a conference at the convention center. I'm walking around downtown, and we happen to cross paths. He goes, "Oh, you're Pastor Doug!" And I'm like, "You know who I am?"

He says, "Pastor Doug, I've been watching your sermons online, and I think you're going to be perfect for our new Avengers movie."

I can't believe what I'm hearing, but my mind immediately jumps to the obvious. He wants me to replace Robert Downey Jr. as Iron Man. I open my mouth to proudly accept, but he continues. "I don't want you to play Iron Man. I don't need you to play Captain America. You're not even going to be Ant Man. I've got the perfect supportive role for you in the film. You're going to be an analyst at Avengers headquarters, and you'll be in a few scenes—maybe get a few lines—and it's going to be great."

At this point in the conversation, I have two options. I can get offended and mad that I'm not a lead role and I could turn him down and walk away. Or I could trust that he knows the best role for me. I could accept the supportive role with enthusiasm, grateful to be part of the story.

We face the same two options in our spiritual lives. We can be supporting actors in God's story—the biggest blockbuster hit of all time. Or we can walk away, angry that we're not the main attraction.

God's movie is going to continue with or without us. It has no beginning, and it has no end. It is the story of the universe, and God is inviting us to participate.

Adam and Eve were given a really great role. They managed creation. In their episode, spiritual warfare interfered. The serpent deceived them, convincing them that they deserved to be the stars of the movie. He convinced them they could be gods. This is the very lie that Satan believed himself. Look at his origin story in Isaiah 14:13–14. Satan says, "I will ascend to the heavens; I will raise my throne above the stars of God; I will sit enthroned on the mount of assembly, on the utmost heights of Mount Zaphon. I will ascend above the tops of the clouds; I will make myself like the Most High" (NIV).

Satan wanted to be a god. That sounds a lot like pride.

Oftentimes, self-rejection is an outer-layer symptom of a deeper layer of pride. People feel self-rejection because they believe that they deserve more. They believe they're better than others, more worthy than others. And they get angry when the rest of the world doesn't agree. Prideful people believe that everything is about them, when in reality, they haven't embraced the role handed them. They think they should be Iron Man when God has a perfect spot for them as a headquarters analyst.

Embracing your role doesn't mean that you settle for less. When you embrace your role, however big or small, you free yourself up to experience your best life possible. You bring glory to God while living out your utmost potential. Sounds pretty worthwhile, doesn't it?

While some of us demand to be lead stars, there are others who feel pretty content with how their movie is going. They think, "I have a good reputation, great social media presence. I look good, I connect with people well, and I'm making good money. Things are going great with my family and my relationships. So why would I want to let God be the star of my movie when my movie is already a success? Why would I want to waste time going to church, praying, focusing on God? I haven't needed Him so far; why would I need him now?"

These people may have a great movie, but they're missing one thing. Our individual lives here on earth make up for a small fraction of the entire saga of the world. Our stories are short stories in the epic story of humankind.

Let me illustrate it like this. Who was the tenth president in the United States? Most of us can't answer this without running through the names of presidents one through nine. The tenth president was John Tyler. He isn't a household name, and yet he was president of the United States.

If most of the world can't remember John Tyler, what makes us think that people will remember us after we've passed on? What makes us think that we'll leave a legacy that will still be talked about one hundred, two-hundred years down the line?

God's story will continue on while our individual stories fade over time. This is why it's so much better to be part of His movie than to cling to our own.

Think about the fact that celebrities' popularity fades. Award-winning journalist John Dickerson points this out in his book *Jesus Skeptic* when he mentions how Kanye West collaborated on a song with Paul McCartney of the Beatles. McCartney is one of the most famous celebrities of the twentieth century, yet after the song came out, a younger American tweeted, "I don't know who Paul McCartney is, but Kanye is going to give this man a career with this new song!" That was a real tweet. Dickerson wrote, "Paul McCartney is one of the most famous people of the last fifty years. He is still alive, and already a new generation of young adults does not know who he is. This is just the way history works. The sands of time bury everyone."[19]

Unlike other notable celebrities and world leaders, Jesus' influence continues to increase. There are currently well over 2 billion people who claim to follow Jesus.[20] This is currently more than any other religion. John Dickerson pointed out that "whether you believe Jesus is God or not, whether you believe in the spiritual realm or not, it is a fact of history that the year of your birth is based on the year of Jesus's birth. The entire globe today uses a calendar that is based on the estimated birth year of Jesus of Nazareth. No other figure in history can make that kind of claim about the global calendar. None."[21] Clearly to align oneself with Jesus is to align with the winning story of history.

Do Not Customize God

Self-rejection is a dangerous state of mind that can bring hurt, suffering, pain, and ultimately, it causes us to leave God's story. When we don't believe we have anything to offer—or conversely, when we believe we have *all the answers*—we reject our role in God's movie.

No story illustrates this more than the story of Pharaoh in Exodus.

Pharaoh thought he was a god. When Moses, a man who had submitted his life to God and accepted his role, went to him and demanded that he free Moses' people, Pharaoh refused. Pharaoh didn't care what God wanted. He didn't care what was best for the people. He believed it was all about him and his desires.

The Bible tells us in Exodus 14:17–18, God said: "I will harden the hearts of the Egyptians so that they will go in after them. And I will gain glory through Pharaoh and all his army, through his chariots and his horsemen. The Egyptians will know that I am the LORD when I gain glory through Pharaoh, his chariots and his horsemen" (NIV).

The only reason that you and I know about this pharaoh is because he's a part of the story of God. He played a role whether he wanted to or not. It could have been a positive role of redemption. Instead it was a role of a man who lost it all.

We have the same choice to make. If self-rejection is holding you back from choosing to be part of God's movie, then it is time to root out those thoughts. By loving God, you will learn to love yourself *and* others. You will move from self-hate and self-pride to self-acceptance. And you will play the role that you were made for.

In order to thoroughly root out the self-rejection you may be feeling, go ahead and pray this prayer out loud:

Dear Heavenly Father, I confess and renounce *self-rejection*. I ask You that I be released from any guilt or shame associated with the self-rejection. In Jesus' name and by His blood, I cancel Satan's authority over me from the *self-rejection*. In Jesus' name, I command *self-rejection* to leave me now, with all its works and effects.

Holy Spirit, I invite You to fill me and heal me from the deepest roots of *self-rejection*. Holy Spirit, please give me a word, picture, or thought about my role in the great story of God.

Take a moment to listen and reflect in stillness.

WORKBOOK

Chapter Five Questions

Question: Look at the indicators of self-rejection: self-pity, self-humiliation, self-focus, competition and comparison, talking too much or too little, religious legalism, and bodily abuse. Are any of these present in your life, and if so, how do they point back to a deeper issue of self-rejection? Do you see any of these indicators in the lives of your loved ones?

_____

_____

_____

_____

_____

_____

_____

_____

Question: How do you think God sees you? What do your emotions tell you, and what does the Bible tell you? How can you move from basing your acceptance on feelings to basing it on the authority of Scripture?

_____

_____

_____

_____

_____

_____

_____

_____

_____

_____

_____

Question: Have you embraced your role as a "supporting actor" in the epic story of God, or are you trying to be the star of your own show? What examples from your life support that answer? How can you keep your focus on God's bigger plan instead of your personal goals and desires?

_____

_____

_____

_____

_____

_____

_____

_____

_____

_____

_____

_____

Action: We grow in our love for God and desire to fulfill His role for our lives as we spend time getting to know Him. Commit to a daily time of fellowship with the Lord. When and where can you best do this? What specific tools will help you in focusing on Him (Bible, devotional, prayer journal, Christian music, etc.)?

Chapter Five Notes

CHAPTER SIX

Deal with Counterfeit Spirituality

When I was in college, I did a summer youth ministry internship at my home church. I worked with my youth pastor, Phil Dietz. Phil mentored me in my younger years in the area of spiritual warfare. Some of the principles I learned during those years can be found in Phil's book *Authority and Power: Spiritual Warfare: From Darkness Into Light.*[22] During the internship, I was there to help shepherd the students, and one of the students who needed quite a bit of our time was Alex.

Alex was involved in Satanism, and he and his coven had a strategy to infiltrate Christian churches, kidnap kids, and molest them. We had caught him with the intent to do this and reported him to the police. So, needless to say, Alex didn't like us very much, and he certainly didn't want our help. He and his coven would sacrifice animals and throw them on our cars. They'd threaten us and malign us. They did everything they could to get under our skin.

I was staying with my parents at this time, and one night, someone entered the house, turned a hairdryer on high heat, and left it in a place where over time, it would have started a fire. By the grace of God, we found it and turned it off.

After the summer internship was over with, I went back to college, only to keep getting calls from Satanists harassing me. Then I met this guy I like to call Jesus Fish Belt Buckle Guy, because he had a belt buckle in the shape of a Jesus fish. Belt Buckle Guy was always asking me if we could get together and pray. I'd agree, but something always got in the way and prevented me from following through. I found out later from one of the professors—who had a background in intelligence and received the info from a former work colleague—that Belt Buckle Guy was actually a drug dealer and a Satanist.

Test the Spirits

The demonic is all around us. It is active and meddling in your life *today*. I don't want you to be scared and unsure like I was. I want you to be equipped to help yourself and others deal with this very dangerous reality. Sure, most situations that you'll run into won't involve Satanism and the occult. But that doesn't mean that you should take things any less seriously.

This may be somewhat familiar to you. Perhaps you grew up in a spiritual environment that taught and trained you about the demonic realm. If this was your background, then congratulations! You already know how serious this stuff can get.

Perhaps you embrace what we'll call "Western naturalism," which means you only believe what you can observe, and you've been led to believe that all this talk of demons is just superstition. I know what some of you are thinking: "Yeah, all this is for those ignorant, superstitious people who believe that the Chupacabra, Bigfoot, and championship wrestling are real."

Even if you don't believe in the demonic, I'm sure you're astute enough to observe the evil and oppression in our world. I'd suggest something is influencing these realities. In my travels, I've found that it's common for people in Africa, Central America, and South America to believe in the spiritual realm. Hopefully, those of you who are open-minded can consider that maybe our friends from other parts of the world have been exposed to some things we haven't. Americans and Western Europeans are often culturally narrow when it comes to the spiritual realm.

You may be one of the many, many Christians who grew up in a home that didn't offer any training or teaching on the spiritual realm. If this is you, then welcome into the fold. You're about to absorb a lot of information that may seem odd, but you need to know it.

If you didn't fit into either of the above upbringings,

then perhaps you came from a home in which any kind of spirituality was embraced. New Age, voodoo, anything that involved spirits and power and an unseen realm—all of this was fair game for you. People who grew up in homes such as this oftentimes don't see the danger lurking in the demonic. They tend to view the spiritual realm as something that they can tap into for a boost of power. But there is great danger in that approach.

In 1 John 4:1, John wrote, "Dear friends, do not believe every spirit, but test the spirits to see whether they are from God, because many false prophets have gone out into the world" (NIV).

In light of this text, and many others that we're going to study, I want to submit this one simple idea to you, regardless of your upbringing and background. *We are to test the spirits with power, perspective and process.* Here's what I mean by that.

A friend of mine came to a place in his life where he was willing to test the spirits. In meditative sessions, he went back to a time in his life when he had seen a dark, shadowy figure in his room. It scared him, so he told his mom. His mom went and told the people at the Catholic church that they were attending at the time. People from the church came over, and they put an egg underneath his bed. His mom also put a sheet over his face, and was told by a curandero to spew brandy in his face.

A curandero is a mystical healer. They are viewed by the Catholic church as dangerous and demonic, but for some reason this church embraced them.

Curanderos take bits and pieces of the Bible and mix Christian spirituality with pagan forms of spirituality to supposedly help people, and they oftentimes use herbs and eggs as part of their rituals.

Of course evil spirits are not afraid of herbs and eggs. They are afraid of the inspired Holy Spirit-filled word of God. They're afraid of the blood of Jesus and the cross of Christ and the truth of God's Word. But curanderos are very common in some cultures, and many times Christ-followers don't understand the danger of utilizing them.

My friend told me that when they placed the egg under the bed, it was raw. The next morning, that egg was cooked. The problems seemed to stop. The dark, shadowy figure was no longer there.

Or was it?

My friend eventually became a raging alcoholic. He traces many of the spiritual problems that he had years later, back to that encounter. Did the shadowy figure leave? Or did it do a better job of not being seen?

You may have attended a church that told you never to question anything, but they were wrong. As Christ-followers, we are questioners and we are testers. We are to question and dig into what we are told. It doesn't matter if we're taught something from a pastor, priest, rabbi, or Jedi—we're testers. We are to test the things that are handed to us as fact. We are to work through the spiritualities that we've embraced knowingly and unknowingly.

And we test with power, perspective, and process.

Testing with Power

First, let's test the spirits with power. Paul wrote about spiritual warfare in Ephesians 6:10–12, saying, "A final word: be strong in the Lord and in his mighty power. Put on all of God's armor so that you will be able to stand firm against all the strategies of the devil. For we are not fighting against flesh-and-blood enemies, but against evil rulers and authorities of the unseen world, against mighty powers in this dark world, and against evil spirits in the heavenly places" (NLT).

Paul wanted it to be clear that a very real spiritual war is going on. We can't see it, but it's there and we have to combat it with spiritual weapons.

It makes me think back to when I was a kid. My dad had property that was an hour outside of town. When we'd go hiking through the woods there, he would always take his trusty little pistol with him. I remember one day, we came to a ravine, small enough that I could jump to the other side into a pile of leaves. My dad stopped me.

Like a sheriff in a Western movie, he pulled his pistol out and shot at the pile. Now my dad was a marksman in the Army. His shots were perfect every time! He went to the other side of the ravine, took a stick, and fished out a cottonmouth snake with three bullet holes in its head.

My dad knew about the unseen dangers of this world. He knew to bring a weapon, and to use that weapon before taking a literal leap of faith.

God wants the same for us. He wants us to be aware of the unseen war that wages and to hone our skill with the weapons He's given us, prayer and Scripture. These are the two main tools we have to test with power and take back control from the demonic.

Testing with Perspective

Let's look at how we test the spirits with perspective.

I used to go to the roller-skating rink in middle school. You'd have to pay for a certain amount of time, and then you'd have to wait for your session before you could start skating.

One night, we were waiting for our turn when these high schoolers from a rival school started picking a fight. They were talking trash, and we were just standing there, taking it. I looked through the glass to the roller-skating rink (probably praying to God that time would speed up), and there was my friend Alan Larkin. I pointed him out to my school friends.

As soon as the high schoolers heard that I knew Alan, they left. You see, Alan was one of those guys who developed more quickly than the rest of us. In seventh grade, he looked like he was twenty-five years old and in the special forces! We were just in awe of how he could use nunchucks. He'd swing those things around like it was second nature. He loved to fight and seldom lost.

Hearing his name put fear in the guys who were bullying us, and that same thing happens in the spiritual realm. Luke 10:17–20 says, "When the seventy-two disciples returned, they joyfully reported to him, 'Lord, even the demons obey us when we use your name!' 'Yes,' he told them, 'I saw Satan fall from heaven like lightning! Look, I have given you authority over all the power of the enemy, and you can walk among snakes and scorpions and crush them. Nothing will injure you. But don't rejoice because evil spirits obey you; rejoice because your names are registered in heaven'" (NLT).

Jesus balances the odds. Because of Him, we have power and authority over the demonic realm. But don't get too uppity about it! I cringe when I hear well-meaning Christians talk trash about the devil. They boast, "I'm a demon slayer. Better watch out Satan; I just woke up!"

I think of the seven sons of Sceva who used Jesus' name (Acts 19:11–20). Those demons said, "We know about Jesus, we heard of Paul, but we don't know who you are." The demons won that day even though people had used Jesus' name!

It's a matter of spiritual pride. Jude warned us about this in Jude 1:8–9 (NIV), saying:

> ...these ungodly people pollute their own bodies, reject authority and heap abuse on celestial beings. But even the Archangel Michael, when he was disputing with the devil about the body of Moses, did not himself dare to condemn him for slander, but said, "The Lord rebuke you!" Yet these people slander whatever they do not understand, and the very things that they do understand by instinct—as irrational animals do—will destroy them.

We need to speak softly but carry a big stick. We do have power and authority, but it's only by the grace of God. If He isn't with us, we have nothing! We must go into these encounters with humility of the spirit.

Testing with Process

Last, let's look at testing the spirits with process. We've seen that we have power over the demonic. We have weapons that can do damage in the spiritual realm. We have a new perspective because of Jesus' name. But we also have to follow a process.

There's a story in Mark 9 about a kid with a demon spirit on him. The disciples were fired up about their new-found power to cast out demons when they came upon this kid who couldn't talk because of the demon living in him. Of course, the child's father was upset, not sure what to do or how to manage, and so the disciples offered to cast out the demon.

Only problem was, nothing happened.

Embarrassed, they walked away with their tail between their legs. Mark 9:28 says, "Afterward, when Jesus was alone in the house with his disciples, they asked him, 'Why couldn't we cast out that evil spirit?' Jesus replied, 'This kind can be cast out only by prayer'" (NLT).

There was something wrong in their process that kept them from understanding how to deal with this particular kind of spirit.

In the mid-2000s, I was assisting one of my spiritual warfare mentors, Miriam Callahan. Miriam outlined her process for emotional freedom in *The H2O Workbook: A Biblical Path to Hope, Heal & Overcome for the Thirsty Soul.*[23] At the time, we were dealing with a young woman who had been abused in satanic rituals. Crystal had grown up in a home where her dad, a Bexar County Sheriff's officer, was also a closet Satanist. Throughout her life, he had used her for ritual abuse.

Her grandfather was a Baptist pastor at a small Baptist church on the south side of San Antonio. They had a secret room in this church where they would do satanic sacrifices on the church communion table.

Crystal became so fed up with the abuse, she told her Christian schoolteacher, and that teacher called the authorities. They arrested Crystal's dad and put him in prison. I believe he's in prison to this day. The grandfather was elderly, and he ended up passing away before facing legal consequences.

After all this had transpired, she came to get help from us. I was able to witness her enter into a great, new life. She found the freedom and peace she had always craved. She's married, living under a new name, and doing what she loves to do.

It's an impactful story that is not easy to boil down to a few paragraphs. But it was a process! Hours of therapy, hours of prayer, setback after setback and then finally steps forward.

It's easy to focus on the highlight reel, to go for the winning touchdown right away. But true healing takes effort. For Crystal, it took several of us to pour into her over the course of years.

Most of the freedom that people experience comes as a result of a long process. We see this in Mark 9. Jesus had a process that He went through. It's not an exhaustive process, and the process can change. You also have to be open to the Spirit's movement. That said, we can pull general guidelines from the life of Jesus.

Step 1: Jesus had a lifestyle of prayer and fasting. Mark 9:29 says, "This kind can be cast out only by prayer" (NLT). Some translations will tack on "and fasting" because it was assumed in that day that fasting always went with prayer. Oftentimes, you'll find that if you're in the midst of a fast, you are more prepared for a spiritual warfare encounter.

Step 2: Jesus confirmed belief. Mark 9:21–24 (NIV) reads:

> *Jesus asked the boy's father, "How long has he been like this?"*
>
> *"From childhood," he answered. "It has often thrown him into fire or water to kill him. But if you can do anything, take pity on us and help us."*
>
> *"'If you can'?" said Jesus. "Everything is possible for one who believes."*
>
> *Immediately the boy's father exclaimed, "I do believe; help me overcome my unbelief!"*

That's a great, honest prayer, and it was exactly what Jesus was looking for. There are times I don't know what to do. In those times, I try to believe, but "Lord, will you please help my unbelief?" Jesus helps you and fills in the blanks. He just wants you to be honest with Him and to look to Him for the answer—not yourself. He wants to know that you believe.

Step 3: Jesus explored the person's past. He explored the boy's past in verse 21: "Jesus asked the boy's father, 'How long has he been like this?' 'From childhood,' he answered" (NIV).

I can only assume the boy experienced something very traumatic that gave more power to this demonic spirit and allowed the spirit to take root for such a long time.

At one point Crystal explained to me that when

someone has been harmed as a child or has gone through a traumatic event, it can take years—*decades*—for them to process it and move to a place of freedom, healing, and normalcy.

That's why Jesus wants to dig into the past. He wants to explore what happened so that we can come to a place of freedom.

If you went through painful childhood events, I want to encourage you to stick with the process. Stick with coming to church and hearing the Word of God. Stick to worship that will help you feel more normal and spiritually healthy. Stick with your spiritual tribes that you're involved with at church—your small group of people who are praying for you. Stick with your recovery process and counseling. If you decide to dig into your layers at some point, stick with that, too.

And know that all of this takes time.

Some people give up because they're expecting magic, not biblical spirituality. Some people just want someone to smack them on the forehead and knock them backwards in church, when really, in the long run, that may not help them.

Can God do it in a moment? Sure He can. But most of the time it takes a process.

Step 4: Jesus identified the spirit by name. In the medical field, we have to diagnose things and give them a name so that we know how to treat illness. In verse 25, Jesus "rebuked the impure spirit. 'You deaf and mute spirit,' he said, 'I command you, come out of him and never enter him again'" (NIV).

Maybe you need to name something today that is

giving you trouble.

If you read through Acts, there's a story where a group of people had to get rid of their occult books and objects (Acts 19:19). These things gave rights to dark and demonic spirits in their life, so they had to get rid of them.

When was the last time you took an inventory of your home? What objects give you unease? I've seen enough over the years to know that these kinds of things have negative effects: spirit guides, horoscopes, new age spirituality, Kabbalah, curandero, Santeria, Scientology, out-of-body experiences, channeling, talking to the dead, spells, curses, occult games, divination, voodoo, witchcraft, astral projection, palm readers, tarot cards, paganism, and fortune tellers.

Participating in these things is dangerous. And if you have done so, it's time to pray, to renounce these things by name, to remove them from your life, and to ask for God's Holy Spirit to fill you and guide you. And then, you simply need to accept that you are forgiven.

As we are forgiven, God by His Spirit sets us free. He gives us authority, but we must use it wisely. We must follow the process and the steps.

Take Up Your Sword

The demon world is very real. It offers a counterfeit version of faith and power, but it cannot stand up to the pure truth of Jesus Christ.

God has given all that we need to be able to withstand these attacks from counterfeit spirituality. We must be smart! And we must understand that this battle may take years. It's not going to be won overnight.

I encourage you to root out the things in your life that pull you toward the demonic. Take up your spiritual weapons and join me in testing the spirits in power, perspective, and process.

If you have willingly or unwillingly been involved in some type of counterfeit spirituality, let's deal with it in prayer. As you read this chapter, perhaps a particular spiritual practice or experience felt unusually highlighted in your mind. That's very likely a practice or experience you can pray about right now.

Look over the prayer below and place the counterfeit spiritual practice in the appropriate blank as you pray the following prayer out loud:

> Heavenly Father, I confess participating in _____.
> I renounce it as a counterfeit. I pray that You will fill me with Your Holy Spirit so that I may be guided by You. Thank You that in Christ I am forgiven.

Now, make the following declarations of new identity out loud:

> Evil has *no* right to me! (1 John 5:18)

> I have authority over demons! (Mark 6:7)

> Greater is He who is in me then he who is in the world! (1 John 4:4)

I have on the full armor of God! (Ephesians 6:11)

The enemy must flee from me! (James 4:7)

WORKBOOK

Chapter Six Questions

Question: What has been your experience with demonic influences? Did you grow up exposed to these things, or completely unaware of them? Do you have any past experiences that you suspect may have created a demonic stronghold in your life?

_____

_____

_____

_____

_____

_____

_____

_____

_____

Question: Have you ever witnessed someone boasting about their power over Satan and his realm? Maybe this even took the form of a Christian song or phrase. What are some scriptures that you can speak when you are confronted by the forces of darkness? How will they help you to keep the right perspective of recognizing your need for God's power and protection?

_____

_____

_____

_____

_____

_____

_____

_____

_____

_____

_____

Question: Look back at your answer to the first question in Chapter One, regarding your areas of brokenness. Are you expecting a quick fix to each of these, or are you committed to the long process of healing? What specific steps do you need to take (prayer and fasting, confirming belief, exploring the past, identifying the evil) to keep moving forward in the process?

_____

_____

_____

_____

_____

_____

_____

_____

_____

_____

_____

_____

Action: Are there any areas where you have let demonic influences into your life? Besides obvious things such as participation in a satanic ritual or new age spirituality, be sure to evaluate your games, books, movies, and friends. Are there any areas of "fun" or "entertainment" that you need to remove from your life? If you are uncertain remember to use your powerful tools of prayer and Scripture to evaluate.

Chapter Six Notes

_____

_____

_____

_____

_____

_____

_____

_____

_____

_____

_____

_____

_____

_____

_____

_____

_____

_____

_____

_____

_____

_____

CHAPTER SEVEN

Take Nature's Medicine

Most people love animals or nature. They like going to the beach, going out on the rivers or the trails. The reason we have such an affinity for nature, animals, and all of creation is that they're a pathway to God. Nature points us toward God. It is a spiritual pathway, and we see this in Romans 1:19–20, which says, "They know the truth about God because he has made it obvious to them. For ever since the world was created, people have seen the earth and sky. Through everything God made, they can clearly see his invisible qualities—his eternal power and divine nature. So they have no excuse for not knowing God"

(NLT).

Creation actually helps us to see, experience, and know God! But it's also designed to help us heal, physically and mentally. God infused nature with remedies that we can use for healing as we continue this journey of mental health.

Natural Remedies

Imagine being with your dog or cat, or another animal that brings you joy. You love being around that animal, and science shows us why. Petting a dog or cat releases oxytocin, which slows your heart rate and breathing. It calms you down. It also boosts your beta endorphins, the chemical associated with the runner's high. It releases dopamine, the reward hormone. And it also releases serotonin, just like most antidepressants are designed to do. Petting a dog is, essentially, an antidepressant.

Cat owners enjoy a 30-percent reduction in heart attack risk. Fish aquariums are calming and help lower blood pressure. Pet-assisted therapies help troubled children, people with autism, and people who suffer from post-traumatic stress.[24]

In His master plan, God created nature and animals to assist in our mental health. There are things all around us specifically designed to normalize our brain chemistry, and we see time and again in the Bible when God used nature—animals, especially—to aid mankind.

God put animals in the garden with Adam and Eve. God put animals directly into the ark with Noah. When Jesus was born, He was surrounded by animals in the manger, and during His earthly ministry, Jesus taught that not even a sparrow falls to the ground without the Father's care (Matthew 10:29). God sees the importance of animals and nature.

Now, I'm not promising you that if you go on a camping trip, you're going to be healed of bipolar disorder. There are many facets to healing that oftentimes include medications and counseling. What I am suggesting is that if we can have regular doses of nature in our lives, it can lead toward better mental health.

Nature and Rest

When you go back to Genesis, early in the garden, the first commandment that was given to the humans was to tend the garden and take care of it (Genesis 2:15). Further into the Old Testament of the Bible, there is a command for sustainability. Leviticus 25:2 says, "The land itself must observe a Sabbath rest before the LORD every seventh year" (NLT). Part of sustainability was for Old Testament farmers to stop and let the land rest every so many years.

And 2 Chronicles 7:14 says, "If my people, who are called by my name, will humble themselves and pray and seek my face and turn from their wicked ways, then I will hear from heaven, and I will forgive their sin and will heal their land" (NIV). Later when the people refused to give the land a rest, the Lord had His way. Second Chronicles 36:21 reads, "So the message of the LORD spoken through Jeremiah was fulfilled. The land finally enjoyed its Sabbath rest, lying desolate until the seventy years were fulfilled, just as the prophet had said" (NLT).

At the time of the writing of this book, COVID-19 has affected people in such a way that there are fewer cars on the road, planes in the sky, and factories pouring out smoke. Although the COVID-19 crisis is a tragedy, there may be a silver lining. Due to people being forced to give the land a sabbath rest, the sky is visible in Los Angeles. After years of failed attempts to get the panda bears in the Hong Kong Zoo to mate, Ying Ying and Le Le finally succeeded in mating naturally.[25]

There's a connection between our healing and the healing of the land, the healing of the environment. We affect nature, and nature affects us. This is part of God's wonderful, perfect plan.

The problem, though, is that we aren't spending time in nature anymore. According to the Environmental Protection Agency, the average American spends 93% of their lives indoors. When you break that down, 87% of life is being spent inside a building, 6% is spent in an automobile or transportation, and only 7% of our lives is spent in nature.[26] I am here to tell you that God created us to be outside more than that.

Neuroscientist Dr. Andrea Michelli says that there are two positive effects of a single exposure to nature. If you go outside in your garden or spend time in the yard, you'll get the benefits of nature for seven hours after you go inside. The second thing she noted is that those who are more prone to mental illness need nature more than the rest of us.[27] So if you have a potential leaning toward depression or anxiety, the outdoors can help move you toward healing.

God didn't give us nature to burden us with wondering if we've spent enough time outdoors. He gave us nature to help us. And there are practical steps we can take to reignite our connection with the world around us.

- You can form a group of friends to meet you at the park and pray.
- You can study the Bible outside.
- You can go for a run or walk.
- You can open your curtains to let a little more sunshine in.
- Create a space in your yard that invites you to spend time there.
- Start a garden.
- Do landscaping.
- Adopt a pet. Set up a fish aquarium.
- Ride your bike to work, to the store, to the library—whatever's practical.
- Shoot hoops, go ice skating, go skiing, or hike the trails.
- Go outside to pick up roadside trash.
- Visit a new park.

Whatever it is that gets you excited to be outside, grab hold of it and make it part of your routine. I encourage you to take pictures of your time, share those pictures with others to inspire them to experience some of nature's medicine, and then shut your phone down so that you can fully take in the remedies God has provided.

Significant Trees

Throughout the Bible, our relationship with God is described in terms of gardens and vines, rivers, trees, light, soil, and water, but I want to call attention to three specific trees that mark important points in Scripture.

The Bible story begins in Genesis with Adam and Eve in the Garden of Eden. In that garden, God made different kinds of trees: "The LORD God made all kinds of trees grow out of the ground—trees that were pleasing to the eye and good for food. In the middle of the garden were the *tree of life* and *the tree of the knowledge of good and evil*" (NIV, emphasis added).

In this garden, God warned them not to eat fruit from the tree of knowledge of good and evil. Genesis 2:16–17 says, "And the LORD God commanded the man, 'You are free to eat from any tree in the garden; but you must not eat from the tree of the knowledge of good and evil, for when you eat from it you will certainly die'" (NIV). However, they ate of the tree and were removed from the garden. God posted an angel there so they would not be able to eat from the tree of life (Genesis 3:24).

At the end of the Bible, in Revelation, the tree of life makes another appearance. This tree offers every possible healing we could ever need. Revelation 22:2 says, "On each side of the river stood the tree of life, bearing twelve crops of fruit, yielding its fruit every month. And the leaves of the tree are for the healing of the nations" (NIV).

In our eternity with God, we will have renewed access to the tree of life written about in Genesis and Revelation, because of another significant tree. First Peter 2:24 says, "He himself bore our sins in his body on the tree" (ESV).

Jesus died on the most significant tree, *the cross.*

God, through nature, is showing you that He's here. Through the tree of the cross, He wants to show you that you can have a love relationship with Him, if you only believe that Jesus died on the cross for you.

Through nature, God has provided us incredible healing options, yes. But He also has provided us a way to be with Him forever. Let us think about this as we move toward a lifestyle that incorporates God's natural medicine.

Chapter Seven Questions

Question: Describe in as much detail as you can the most breathtaking part of creation that you have ever seen. How does reliving that moment make you feel? What did that experience reveal to you about the nature of God?

_____

_____

_____

_____

_____

_____

_____

_____

_____

_____

Question: Which parts of creation do you find healing and restorative? Do you enjoy a particular type of landscape, have a favorite pet, or find joy in a certain outdoor hobby? If none of these is a regular part of your life, what is one way you could increase your exposure to the natural world and your understanding of God as the Creator?

_____

_____

_____

_____

_____

_____

_____

_____

_____

_____

_____

Question: How did Jesus demonstrate His love for and power over His creation when He lived on the earth?

_____

_____

_____

_____

_____

_____

_____

_____

_____

_____

_____

Action: Plan a day to have your devotional time in the outdoors. This may take creativity in certain seasons or locations. As much as possible, choose a spot that will offer you inspiring views. If you are able, plan a hike or allow for some extra time to observe the nature around you.

Chapter Seven Notes

_____

_____

_____

_____

_____

_____

_____

_____

_____

_____

_____

_____

_____

_____

_____

_____

_____

_____

_____

_____

_____

_____

_____

_____

CHAPTER EIGHT

Make a Choice to Rejoice

Back when I was in college, I went on a mission trip to an under-resourced part of Mexico. While I was there, I got sick. I was well enough to travel home, but when I got home, my symptoms got worse. I kept deteriorating. I couldn't get out of bed, and I had sores all over the inside of my mouth. I went to the doctor, and he diagnosed me with chronic active Epstein-Barr.

When I got well enough to get out of bed, I could barely function. For a year, I was tired all the time, and it sent me spiraling into depression.

One Sunday at church, there was a guest harp-player

named Greg Buchanan. I'm not really into harp music, but Greg's music was like nothing I had ever heard. It was incredible to see him use his gift. Despite his amazing talent, the thing that affected me most about Greg was something he said. Between songs, he paused and told the congregation, "I deal with depression." Then he smiled widely and added, "But I made the choice to rejoice."

Those words stayed with me. In fact, from that point on, I decided to make the choice to rejoice. Despite my physical weakness, I focused on the positives in my life. Rather than thinking about what I couldn't do, I focused on what I could do.

A couple of years after my choice to rejoice, I went back to my doctor to get tested for Epstein-Barr. My doctor was surprised by my test results. Then he explained that once you're infected, you carry the virus—usually in a dormant state—for the rest of your life. Yet my test revealed that I had no trace of Epstein-Barr in my system. It looked as if I'd never had it. I believe there's healing power in the choice to rejoice.

Happiness and contentment come from a choice. Rejoicing starts in your heart, and then it works its way up to your face and out into your life.

This isn't new science or groundbreaking research. The power of positivity has been around for a long time. Uplifting, positive thoughts can change your brain chemistry. It's not hocus pocus. It's fact! And real biological change in your brain can lead to greater mental health.

The Brain That Changes Itself

Norman Doidge works in a field of science called neuroplasticity. Neuroplasticity means that our thoughts can
change the structure and functions of our brains. People
with problems from strokes, cerebral palsy, and mental illnesses can train other parts of their brain to pick up the
slack through repetitive mental and physical activities. In
his book *The Brain That Changes Itself*, Dr. Doidge dis-
cusses how the brain has the capacity to rewire itself
and/or form new neural pathways.[28]

If we do the work, just like exercise, the work requires
repetition and activity to reinforce new learning. Our
brains are like muscles. Positive thoughts and truths can
literally re-map and rewire us toward peace and mental
health. This isn't naïve optimism. I'm not saying that you
can trick your brain into making you good at basketball. I
like the way the late Zig Ziglar put it: "Positive thinking
won't let you do anything, but it will let you do everything
better than negative thinking."[29] In other words, it means
a life of abundance.

God planned this. Jesus taught us, "I came that [you
might] have life and have it abundantly" (John 10:10 NIV).
He didn't make this statement wondering where abundance was going to come from. He knew that it was
available to us in large amounts, and that by drawing
closer to Him, we would uncover this wealth of healing,
positivity, and mental change that is available to us.

Scarcity and Abundance

I learned a lot about abundance versus scarcity from a guy named Tim Sanders. He wrote a powerful book called *Love Is the Killer App.*[30] In this book, he compares abundance with scarcity. People with a scarcity mindset believe that there's not enough to go around. That's why they hold so tightly to what they have. Those of us who operate in abundance say there's plenty for everyone.

It's like the news. People gravitate toward negative news. They believe the world is falling apart, and so they grab hold of news pieces that contribute to their pre-set mindset. Consequently, we have a news media full of negativity. Positive news stories are extremely rare.

I used to work for a very successful company in IT. I remember one manager who told a group of new sales staff to be wary of customers because "all buyers are liars." This created a dysfunctional relationship between the people who sold and people who were trying to buy the products. It immediately created scarcity and mistrust.

On the other hand, you have companies like Southwest Airlines. They've expunged negativity from their corporate culture, and before the COVID-19 pandemic, they had been profitable since 1973.[31] That is hard to do in the airline industry, where companies are going bankrupt all the time. They've succeeded because of a mentality of abundance. They believe that goodness and kindness is abundant—there's enough to go around.

Scarcity people always operate from a mindset that they have to squeeze all they can out of the people in their lives.

Abundance people operate from a mindset that they can give and give and give, and there can still be enough for them at the end of the day. Scarcity people rotate through friendships and relationships. Abundance people always have room for relationship.

When we operate in abundance in our relationships, we're like gardeners. Over the long haul, we invest in people. Over the long haul, we water and care for the plants in the garden. In the right time, they bear great fruit; they give back some of what we have given them, and the cycle continues. That's abundance for you!

Scarcity people are like butchers because they see people as meat to be consumed. They turn every relationship into a competition. They're competitors, not community builders. They compete because they believe there isn't enough to go around. They're scared to lose their position, their title, their tribe.

In abundance, we create community even with the people that would be perceived as a competitor, because we believe there is enough room for everyone to join the winner's circle.

Thinking in Abundance

Some years ago, Tim Sander shared about a study in which researchers were watching and observing a phone booth.[32] This was back when most people didn't have a phone on them. When someone needed to make a call, they would walk into a small booth where there was a pay phone. They'd insert money, and then make their call.

The researchers were watching the phone booth, and

every so often, they would put a silver dollar in the phone booth. When someone went in to make a phone call, they would find the silver dollar and think, "Oh, silver dollar! Good day for me!"

Then the researchers staged a woman who would walk by the outside of the phone booth and drop all of her papers. They analyzed the people who helped her pick up her papers and found that the people with the silver dollar in the phone booth were more likely to help the woman than the people who did not find a silver dollar in the booth.

The people with the silver dollar were in a mindset of abundance. Something good had just happened to them, so why not help someone in need?

This is the beauty and importance of abundance. It's why we have to train our brains to *think* in abundance.

If you would, focus right now on all the good things you have. Maybe you have a car that you own or a car that you are paying to own one day. Maybe you have a house or a really great apartment. Maybe you have land or a business.

No matter what you have, there are people who have more than you. But focusing on them doesn't do you any good. Focusing on what you have—the car, the apartment, the refrigerator full of food—this creates a mindset of abundance.

You see, abundance people rejoice in what they have. You can rejoice at the fact that you got to enjoy a good, robust cup of coffee this morning while you looked out the window at the birdfeeder. You can rejoice in the fact you got to greet your kids and see them smile, or that you got to see your spouse smile first thing in the morning.

You can rejoice that you're alive today. That you're moving and doing and going. You can rejoice that you have meat on your sandwich—not all parts of the world are able to afford this.

Choosing to rejoice in what you have brings a mindset of abundance.

If you've ever heard stories of the Great Depression, then you'll know it was a time of literal scarcity. There was a woman who lived through it named Sarah. Her family was down to one potato, and they thought they might starve. A neighbor came over and brought an onion. Then another neighbor brought some flour. Before evening, enough neighbors had come over and brought what they could, and everyone was eating potato stew together.

Abundance is what happens when we come together. Most people don't get to experience that because they don't live in abundance. They live in scarcity. They hang onto what they have and protect it. They say, "This onion is all I have, and so I'm going to keep it locked away and safe." And they miss out on the community potluck going on a few doors down.

Letting Go

There was an area of Indonesia that had a problem with monkeys. The animals were ruining farmland, eating and tearing it up. They were hard on the environment, and so the people came up with a solution. The farmers used to blow darts at the monkeys, and the monkeys would fall from the trees and die. But it was never their intention to kill them—they just wanted the animals relocated. So the farmers got clever.

They drilled holes in gourds and hollowed them out. They filled the holes with peanuts and tied the gourds to trees. A monkey would come down from the tree to get the peanuts, but when he put his hand inside to grab the treasure, he'd get stuck. His fist was too large to exit the gourd—and he had no desire to drop the nuts. When he was stuck, the farmer would pop out and catch the monkey in a net. This is how they were able to safely move an entire monkey population!

The monkey got captured because he wouldn't let go. He believed those nuts were more important than his freedom, and so he was captured.

God desires us to be free, not captured like those Indonesian monkeys.

I did a little exercise with my church congregation. I asked them to reach into their pocket, purse or wallet and grab some pocket change. If they didn't have change, they were to grab cash.

I told them to put whatever they grabbed in their hand and make a fist. You'd better believe, many of them started to get a bit uneasy! I could hear them murmuring. I could see them nervously looking around.

I told them on the count of three to open their fist and drop whatever was in their hand onto the floor. It was hard for some of them, but on the three-count, money clattered to the floor of the sanctuary.

Then I told them that if they were comfortable with it, to leave the money there as a donation to a ministry to homeless families. And if they were not comfortable with it, they were more than welcome to discretely retrieve their dollars and cents.

The people in the congregation who operated in a sense of abundance were overjoyed to donate to the cause. They knew that freedom meant letting those peanuts go.

When You Don't Feel Like Rejoicing

You might be reading this and thinking, "Okay, Doug. I get it. Abundance is best, but I just can't shake this scarcity mentality!"

Jeremiah was a prophet who tended to look on the negative side. In Lamentations 3:2–6, he talks about God, saying, "He has driven me away and made me walk in darkness rather than light; indeed, he has turned his hand against me again and again, all day long. … He has besieged me and surrounded me with bitterness and hardship. He has made me dwell in darkness like those long dead" (NIV).

There's no denying it. Jeremiah had bad days, and he embraced those bad days. He didn't always feel like choosing to rejoice.

My counseling mentor, Miriam Callahan, explained to me that depression and bad feelings are like waves in the ocean. Sometimes you feel like you can't breathe. But in those moments, you just have to endure the waves.

Jeremiah's raw honesty was clearly that of a man caught in a wave. But here's the good news: that wave didn't last forever.

In Lamentations 3:21–23, Jeremiah wrote, "Yet this I call to mind and therefore I have hope: because of the

LORD's great love we are not consumed, for his compassions never fail. They are new every morning; great is your faithfulness" (NIV). Even Jeremiah was able to—in his own time—choose to rejoice.

Every morning is a fresh start. Every day is a chance to start again. God's love can often feel trite and cliché, because we talk about it so much, but let me tell you there is nothing trite and cliché about it. Jesus tells us that He leaves the ninety-nine to save the one (Matthew 18:12). That is how crazy in love He is with you. That's how much you mean to Him.

He felt that so intensely about His love for you that He came here and died. You are His child. Would you be willing to come and kneel before Him today? Even if you're in the middle of a wave of depression. Even if you are in a mindset of scarcity. Take a chance. Release your fist and receive true freedom and abundance.

WORKBOOK

Chapter Eight Questions

Question: Describe the most positive person you know. What obstacles does this person face, or what have they faced in the past? What fuels their "choice to rejoice"?

_____

_____

_____

_____

_____

_____

_____

_____

_____

_____

_____

Question: Do you live in a scarcity or abundance mindset? What evidence of this do you see in your daily life? How does your mindset impact your relationships and your outreach? Do you feel free or in bondage in your outlook on life?

_____

_____

_____

_____

_____

_____

_____

_____

_____

_____

_____

_____

Question: What are some practical ways you can allow God to encourage your heart and transform your attitude when you are overwhelmed with depression, discouragement, lack, need, or pain?

_____

_____

_____

_____

_____

_____

_____

_____

_____

_____

_____

_____

Action: In what ways is your life truly blessed with abundance? Make a list of as many blessings as you can think of. How can you give out of your abundance in each of these areas? In what areas have you overlooked your blessings and fallen into a scarcity mindset? Will you now make the decision to rejoice?

Chapter Eight Notes

_____

_____

_____

_____

_____

_____

_____

_____

_____

_____

_____

_____

_____

_____

_____

_____

_____

_____

_____

_____

_____

_____

CONCLUSION

Make a Daily Choice

As our time together comes to a close, I want to make sure you know why I bothered to write this book. Years ago, when I was going through a significant depression, marital problems, a lust addiction, and thoughts of ending my life, I said a dangerous prayer, *"Lord, I give You permission to do whatever it takes to set me free."* After I prayed that prayer, things got worse, as some of my private struggles came to light and I was fired from my beloved ministry job. Now that the real me was exposed to light, the steps of freedom could begin. I made a choice to take those steps day by day, step by step, and moment by moment.

One of the steps I took was seeking help. I was living through the "dark years," in which I felt like a dark cloud of confusion was over me. I needed help. I also felt completely spiritually defeated, so I traveled to another state to submit myself to what's called "Spiritual Freedom Counseling."

A couple of guys led me through an inventory of all my sins, and I confessed them all to God. Then they led me to pray "spiritual warfare" prayers and speak spiritual truth declarations. They asked me to declare these words out loud, "I am not defeated."

With my mind I was thinking the words, *"I am not defeated,"* but to my surprise, my mouth was saying, "I am defeated." The men asked me to try it again—same result. This experience emotionally jolted me! I thought, *"What's going on here?"* My brain was saying, "I am not defeated," but my mouth was outside of my mental control and kept saying, "I am defeated." This was disturbing! It was subtle and strange.

It wasn't like my head was spinning around. It wasn't like I was speaking in a Darth Vader voice. It sounded like a lower version of my voice saying, "I am defeated." Then the two men prayed a "spiritual warfare prayer" over me. After their prayer, they asked me to make the declaration again. Then, finally, I was able to think with my mind and pray with my mouth, "I am *not* defeated."

When I returned home from that "Freedom Counseling," my wife observed me over a period of weeks. I'll never forget her words. She said, "Doug, it seems like you're back to your normal self. It's like the cloud of confusion is gone. You seem clear-minded." That experience was a definite turning point in my life.

Not long after, I was doing my Bible reading one morning and a verse seemed to be unusually highlighted for me. It was Psalm 51:10–13:

Create in me a pure heart, O God, and renew a steadfast spirit within me. Do not cast me from your presence or take your Holy Spirit from me. Restore to me the joy of your salvation and grant me a willing spirit, to sustain me. Then I will teach transgressors your ways, so that sinners will turn back to you.

I prayed that psalm out loud and made it a prayer for my life. A strong thought entered my mind that if God restored my life, I was to dedicate the rest of my life to "teach transgressors his ways" to experience restoration. And I believe it was God speaking to me.

After some time, God restored my mental health, marriage, and ministry, and He set me free from a long-time struggle with lust. Since 2001, I've been very open and honest to people about my struggles, and that has led to conversations with literally thousands of people about their own emotional hurts and addictions. Many of whom have since experienced new levels of restoration and healing.

This has all happened because of God's grace and my choice to "teach transgressors" His ways. If you've read to this point in the book, that commitment has been fulfilled in your reading.

A Way Through

Some of us are dealing with stuff that we didn't choose to deal with. Life happens, and many times we're just along for the ride. We wake up one day and we're a cracked pot, like the one described in the introduction of this book. We're not living up to our full potential, and we don't know what to do about it.

There is a way through the storm. Psalm 118:24 says, "This is the day the LORD has made; we will rejoice and be glad in it" (NLT).

We've been on a journey together, looking at ways that we can grow in our mental health and get over mental illnesses. We've been making the declaration, "I choose to deal with how I feel," and we understand that this is a daily choice.

We've seen that there are many facets of mental illness healing. There's the medical part tied to biology, and that's why some of us need to use medications and seek doctors to help us through. Some of us need counseling and therapy. But we also saw how God needs to be part of our healing process, because there's the spiritual side of things. We talked about the demonic and how our thoughts can make room for some ugly stuff to take root in our lives.

A reminder from 2 Corinthians 10:5 is that "we demolish arguments and every pretension that sets itself up against the knowledge of God, and we take captive every thought to make it obedient to Christ" (NIV). Romans 12:2 says, "Do not conform to the pattern of this world, but be transformed by the renewing of your mind. Then you will be able to test and approve what God's will is—his good, pleasing and perfect will" (NIV).

Our minds are a battlefield! And we have the power to choose God, to choose to rejoice, and to win the war. May God bless you and keep you, and may His glorious face of healing and restoration shine upon you.

REFERENCES

Notes

1. "The Cracked Pot." Bible.org. https://bible.org/illustration/cracked-pot.

2. Bennington, Draven. "Draven Bennington Interview." Toosie N Noosie. Youtube video. September 15, 2017. https://www.youtube.com/watch?v=OJPQkHDvgl0.

3. "The Cracked Pot," Bible.org.

4. "The Cracked Pot," Bible.org.

5. Crabb, Larry. *Connecting: A Radical New Vision.* W Publishing Group, 1997.

6. Crabb, *Connecting*.

7. "Concussions and Traumatic Brain Injury." SPECT Gallery. Amen Clinics. https://www.amenclinics.com/spect-gallery/concussions-traumatic-brain-injury/.

8. Morehead, Daniel. "Winning the Battle of Mental Illness." Hope for Mental Health. Youtube video. February 2, 2016. https://www.youtube.com/watch?v=F3e6m2ySynY.

9. Gallagher, Richard. *Demonic Foes: My Twenty-Five Years As a Psychologist Investigating Possessions, Diabolic Attacks, and the Paranormal.* HarperOne, 2020.

10. Lewis, C. S. *Screwtape Letters.* Zondervan, 2001, p. ix.

11. Lamott, Anne. Traveling Mercies: Some Thoughts on Faith. Pantheon, 1999.

12. Wise, Jeff. "When Fear Makes Us Superhuman." Scientific American. December 28, 2009. https://www.scientificamerican.com/article/extreme-fear-superhuman/.

13. Mathias, Art. *Biblical Foundations for Freedom: Destroying Satan's Lies with God's Truth.* Wellspring Publishing, 2010.

14. Harvard Health Publishing. "Pain, Anxiety, and Depression." Harvard Mental Health Letter. June 5, 2019. https://www.health.harvard.edu/staying-healthy/anxiety_and_physical_illness.

15. Cobain, Kurt. "I Hate Myself and Wanna Die." *The Beavis and Butt-Head Experience.* Geffen, 1993.

16. Clarkson, Kelly. "I Hate Myself for Losing You." *Breakaway.* RCA Records, 2004.

17. Womack, Lee Ann. "I May Hate Myself in the Morning." *There's More Where That Came From.* MCA Nashville, 2005.

18. Giglio, Louie. "Soundtrack." DVD series. Passion Resources.

19. Dickerson, John S. *Jesus Skeptic: A Journalist Explores the Credibility and Impact of Christianity."* Baker Publishing Group, 2019, p. 210.

20. Pew Research Center. "The Future of World Religions: Population Growth Projections, 2010–2050." 2015.

21. Dickerson, *Jesus Skeptic,* p. 219.

22. Dietz, Phil. *Authority and Power: Spiritual Warfare: From Darkness into Light.* Life Training Publishing, 2020.

23. Callahan, Miriam E. *The H2O Workbook: A Biblical Path to Hope, Heal, and Overcome for the Thirsty Soul.* Miriam E. Callahan, 2017.

24. Montgomery, Sy. "Psychological Effects of Pets Are Profound." Boston Globe. January 12, 2015. https://www.bostonglobe.com/lifestyle/2015/01/12/your-brain-pets/geoJHAfFHxrwNS4OgWb7sO/story.html.

25. Cho, Diane J. "The Amazing Ways Animals and the Environment Have Bounced Back Amid Coronavirus Pandemic." People.com, 2020. https://people.com/human-interest/how-coronavirus-pandemic-has-affected-animals-the-environment/?slide=7793066#7793066.

26. Klepeis, Neil E., William C. Nelson, Wayne R. Ott, John P. Robinson, Andy M. Tsang, Paul Switzer, Joseph V. Behar, Stephen C. Hern, and William H. Engelmann. "The National

Human Activity Pattern Survey: A Resource for Assessing Exposure to Environmental Pollutants (NHAPS)." *Journal of Exposure Analysis and Environmental Epidemiology* 11 (2001), p. 3. https://indoor.lbl.gov/sites/all/files/lbnl-47713.pdf.

27. Pritchard, Emma-Louise. "The Mental Health Benefits of Going for a Walk Can Last for 7 Hours, According to Pioneering New Study." Country Living. January 10, 2018. https://www.countryliving.com/uk/wellbeing/news/a180/mental-health-benefits-nature-outdoors-study/.

28. Doidge, Norman. *The Brain That Changes Itself: Stories of Personal Triumph from the Frontiers of Brain Science.* Penguin, 2007.

29. Ziglar, Zig. *Raising Positive Kids in a Negative World.* Thomas Nelson, 2002.

30. Sanders, Tim. *Love Is the Killer App: How to Win Business and Influence Friends.* Three Rivers Press, 2003.

31. Dahl, Darren. "Why Do Southwest Airlines Employees Always Seem So Happy?" Forbes. https://www.forbes.com/sites/darrendahl/2017/07/28/why-do-southwest-airlines-employees-always-seem-so-happy/?sh=566fe1e459b0.

32. Sanders, Tim. "The Lovecat Way." The Leadership Summit 2003. Willow Creek Association.

About the Author

Doug Robins is the Senior Pastor of City Tribe Church in San Antonio, Texas. He's led the church to grow with irreligious and unchurched people. In addition, Doug has grown a church that is ethnically, generationally and economically diverse. His sweet spot is inspiring broken people to be transformed by Christ. Doug often says, "God has a lot of jacked-up kids, and City Tribe is where we all found each other." Whether or not you can attend City Tribe, you can be encouraged by Doug's inspirational messages on YouTube at City Tribe Media, or on the City Tribe Podcast on iTunes or Sound Cloud.

Made in the USA
Monee, IL
24 February 2021

61256330R10085